# Essentials of Qualitative Inquiry

*Qualitative Essentials*

Series Editor
Janice Morse, University of Utah

Qualitative Essentials is a book series providing a comprehensive but succinct overview of topics in qualitative inquiry. These books will fill an important niche in qualitative methods for students and others new to qualitative inquiry who require a rapid but complete perspective of specific methods, strategies, and important topics. Written by leaders in qualitative inquiry, alone or in combination, these books will be an excellent resource for instructors and students from all disciplines. Proposals for the series should be sent to the series editor at explore@LCoastPress.com.

Title from the Qualitative Essentials series:

1. *Naturalistic Observation,* Michael V. Angrosino

# Essentials of Qualitative Inquiry

Maria J. Mayan

Routledge
Taylor & Francis Group

LONDON AND NEW YORK

First published 2009 by Left Coast Press, Inc.

Published 2016 by Routledge
2 Park Square, Milton Park, Abingdon, Oxon OX14 4RN
711 Third Avenue, New York, NY 10017, USA

*Routledge is an imprint of the Taylor & Francis Group, an informa business*

Library of Congress Cataloging-in-Publication Data
Mayan, Maria J.
  Essentials of qualitative inquiry / Maria J. Mayan.
    p. cm. — (Qualitative essentials)
  Includes bibliographical references and index.
  ISBN 978-1-59874-106-3 (hardcover : alk. paper)–ISBN 978-1-59874-107-0 (pbk. : alk. paper)
  1. Ethnology—Qualitative research. 2. Ethnology–Methodology. I. Title.
  GN345.M39 2009
  305.80072'3–dc22
                       2009002322


ISBN 978-1-59874-107-0      paperback
ISBN 978-1-59874-106-3      hardcover

# Table of Contents

# Preface

*The Essentials of Qualitative Inquiry* is the result of doing and teaching qualitative research and learning from remarkable international qualitative scholars. For the past six years, I directed a nationally funded transdisciplinary training program in qualitative inquiry. In this role, I facilitated a weekly seminar in qualitative inquiry. Students have been local and international at the masters, doctoral, and postdoctoral levels from clinical psychology, education, human ecology, nursing, occupational therapy, public health, rehabilitation science, rural sociology, and sociology. My background is a jointly held PhD between human ecology and business. We gather and engage in discussions about the nature of qualitative inquiry. Welcome to my pleasure and pain. It has been one of the most enriching professional experiences I have had and will likely ever have.

Because of my broad qualitative experiences, I wanted to write a book that would be useful to and anchored in the questions of newcomers to qualitative inquiry, regardless of discipline. I also wanted to write the book to share some of the struggles I have had in learning and continually relearning qualitative inquiry. I have tried to convey how I have made sense of some of the arguments and main concerns in the field. I have tried to lay out both sides of a debate. I have incorporated an exercise into each chapter so that some of the content can be applied. But this book is an introduction. For the "stuff" you are deeply interested in, you will need to do further reading, and this book can point you in particular directions.

My hope is that you are as captivated by the process of doing your research as you are with your findings. Let qualitative inquiry enable you to experience your research in its fullness: See it, smell it, taste it, hear it, touch it. Take it all in, let it envelope you, and enjoy the ride.

# Acknowledgments

I must thank some students whom I lured into reading this book. Ashna Rawji-Ruchkall provided some comments on beginning chapters, and Lyndie Shih commented on the book from front to back. Sanchia Lo read, reread, and helped with formatting, figures, tables, and references, and was my supportive sounding board. Moira Calder took on the task of technical editor.

I am indebted to the EQUIPP trainees who have engaged me in some of the most important and challenging discussions of my career. I thank all current and former EQUIPP students for taking me from poststructuralism to grounded theory and back again in sixty seconds flat.

It was a pleasure and privilege working with Mitch Allen and his crew at Left Coast Press.

I am grateful to Jan Morse for teaching me the importance of theory, methods, and learning-by-doing. She created a space for me to become an academic and to have young children. She bought me a comfy nursing chair for my office when kids came along and soothed colicky babies as I pounded out words for a manuscript. She celebrated each success with pizza and cake. She has provided endless encouragement and countless opportunities, including writing this book.

# Introduction to Qualitative Inquiry

Chapter 1 outlines what qualitative inquiry is and what it is not, introduces the concept of methodological coherence and the heuristic of the armchair walkthrough, and concludes with some qualitative "annoyances."

From its formal beginnings in anthropology, qualitative inquiry has contributed to science by making the taken-for-granted world visible in unique and sometimes jarring ways. Researchers who have traditionally avoided qualitative inquiry are beginning to ask qualitative questions; those who have engaged in qualitative inquiry for decades are *troubling* or pushing the boundaries of comfortable or more established qualitative approaches; and researchers in government and community settings are incorporating qualitative inquiry into their systems.

Recently, I was invited to talk about qualitative inquiry to a group of pediatric organ transplant surgeons and specialists. Since the 1960s, astonishing transplant research has been conducted, saving the lives of neonates, infants, and children. In our local hospital we know the number of infants born each year with congenital heart disease and neonatal cardiomyopathy; we know how many infants receive heart transplants each year, we track success rates; and we record infection and rejection rates. But what do all of these numbers mean? I am reminded of Albert Einstein's quote: "Everything that can be counted does not necessarily count; everything that counts cannot necessarily be counted" (Harris, 1995). This quote is said to have been on a sign hanging in his Princeton office. The professional group that I addressed had these questions: Why do some parents choose not to proceed with a transplant? What is a "successful" transplant, and according to whom? Given the likelihood of growth and developmental delays following transplant, do parents ever regret their decision to proceed?

Many people come to qualitative inquiry in this way, wanting to know the stories behind the numbers. The best way to do this, as suggested by Agar and Kozel (1999), is to "go out and listen to the people [to] whom the numbers referred, listen to their words and learn from their actions" (p. 1936). This will enable you to understand why the numbers exist as they do. Agar and Kozel have encouraged us to remember that "each data point is a person with a biography ... who can show and tell what it is in their life that the data point reflects" (p. 1936). Following this advice, then, we could ask: What is the mother's story behind her infant's "successful" heart transplant? See Exercise 1.1: Finding the Story behind the Numbers.

Regardless of whether you are a quantitative researcher who is starting to wonder about the story behind the numbers, a qualitative researcher who will proudly be never anything but, or a mixed-method researcher who is skilled at both approaches, the questions opened up to us through qualitative inquiry can help explain crises, injustices, and everyday life in new and intriguing ways. It may push you into uncomfortable spaces whereby you see things differently. But it is not easy.

I am reminded of this every year when I teach the introductory qualitative course in my faculty. When a student receives a B–, I often hear a complaint: "You can't give me a B–. I am an A+ student, and I have never had a B– before in my life." My reply is consistent: The course is difficult because we have been taught to think quantitatively. Our world is structured quantitatively. We almost intuitively ask: How many and how much? What did you get on your spelling test? What is the interest rate on your five-year mortgage? How much did the groceries cost? Documents report immigration, HIV/AIDS, unemployment, and poverty rates. We are bombarded with and mesmerized by statistics, and quite regularly we partake directly in the generation of them. Surveyors interrupt our evening meals to administer questionnaires using Likert-like scales regarding our music, food, and car choices, where we like to shop, and what we like to buy. We function very well quantitatively; we have to.

Thinking qualitatively is very different, however, and applying a quantitative way of thinking to a qualitative project begets a B–.

## What Is Qualitative Inquiry?

What is qualitative inquiry? I hesitate to include such a heading in this book, as there is likely very little in common among those of us who call ourselves qualitative researchers. I will be brief. I will also try to be broad enough to be inclusive of various histories and perspectives and meaningful to the anthropologists and phenomenologists, whose qualitative history starts in the late 1800s, but narrow enough to provide the person new to qualitative inquiry, such as the pediatric organ transplant surgeons who I addressed, with a sure start.

Qualitative inquiry is primarily naturalistic, interpretive, and inductive. By studying naturally occurring phenomena, qualitative researchers attempt to interpret or make sense of the meaning people attach to their experiences or underlying a particular phenomenon. Qualitative researchers work inductively from individual cases (the data) and not from a preexisting framework or a particular theory. We qualitative researchers must use creativity, sensitivity, and flexibility as we try to make sense of life as it unfolds. Consequently, we are not concerned with the control of particular variables within a setting but instead invite context, complexity, and "confounding variables." This requires patience and the ability to live with enormous amounts of ambiguity.

If you want to study context, analysis must be in-depth and focused on only a small sample or a few individuals' situations, yet data do not come only from individuals' situations or stories (i.e., interviews). Qualitative data are found in various empirical sources (movement, image, text, sound, etc.). Hence, qualitative researchers aim not to limit a phenomenon—make it neat, tidy, and comfortable—but to break it open, unfasten, or interrupt it so that a description of the phenomenon, in all of its contradictions, messiness, and depth, is (re)presented. The (re)presentation of the data from a qualitative study can take many forms, from art, music, poetry, novels, performance, and personal biographies to taxonomies, models, and theories; it can also be used to develop surveys and instruments and to generate hypotheses.

As this book is being written, my colleagues and I are finalizing a logo for a qualitative training program called EQUIPP,[1] of which I am the director. Using a participatory design, five of us, along with a graphic designer, gathered together over a period of months to create a visual representation of qualitative research. Through the use of projective techniques, we tried to verbally and later visually "define" qualitative inquiry.

Below is a glimpse into some of our conversations,[2] which led to the development of the logo.

> *Humanness* is a key element of qualitative research. Qualitative researchers enjoy living and learning with people to collectively make sense of our worlds. Qualitative research is not only done with people, it is also accomplished through people from different disciplines with different perspectives and life histories. Metaphors of flowers, trees, horizons, and wild horses capture the spirit and life inherent in this dimension of qualitative research. Qualitative researchers are likened to *explorers* because our curiosity can take us into uncharted and mysterious territory. Sometimes this is uncomfortable and dangerous, as it would be to explore a cave or a deep jungle. In other ways, it can take a researcher into vast and open landscapes such as prairies. All of these spaces for exploration take a researcher into alien lands but always with the goal of discovering the depth and breadth of human experience and extending the boundaries of the spaces that different people inhabit.

**EQUIPP**

FIGURE 1.1:
EQUIPP LOGO

> The *complexity* of qualitative research can be represented by a kaleidoscope: multifaceted, ever evolving, and colorful with bright and bold colors. As the researcher moves around, the shapes and meanings change, making qualitative research seem messy and ambiguous at times. The researcher uses all five senses to work creatively and flexibly through a process that is rarely neat and linear. Connecting with people, taking risks to explore new ground, and managing the unpredictable nature of qualitative research can produce rich and important knowledge about our social world. This is captured graphically in Figure 1.1.

This description and illustration might sound and look somewhat chaotic, but qualitative inquiry is a scientific pursuit with certain theoretical underpinnings and methods, each requiring a particular and systematic yet flexible approach to the question or phenomenon of interest (see methodological coherence, below). It is not airy-fairy, soft, or sappy. Moreover, it is not inferior to quantitative inquiry. Both qualitative inquiry and quantitative inquiry are important and will illuminate a phenomenon, but they will illuminate different aspects of it. Regardless of how you align yourself, qualitatively or quantitatively, you should not quarrel about which is better. That argument is so old that I am mortified when I still hear it.

# Methodological Coherence and the Armchair Walkthrough

I work on numerous multidisciplinary research teams, teach students from various disciplines, and work in a variety of community settings that are often dominated by quantitative inquiry. I am patient when explaining what I do as a qualitative researcher, although this is trying at times. Nevertheless, I am sympathetic when colleagues outside of qualitative inquiry who truly are trying to understand and appreciate qualitative work conclude that it is unscientific and generally poor in quality. Many times I would have to agree: Some of the qualitative research published has been conducted very badly. This raises the question of why that is.

Part of the problem is made clear to me in discussions that ensue after I ask students what they want to do. I will often hear something like: "I like postmodernism. I think I will use phenomenology, I will conduct semistructured interviews with about seventeen people. I will use constant comparison for analysis and have a theory at the end of it." The culprit, in this case, is a lack of methodological coherence. Unfortunately, some studies that are methodologically incoherent are published.

Methodological coherence will ensure congruence between your epistemological and ontological viewpoint, your theoretical position/ perspective, the method you choose, your research question, and so on. (Ontology and epistemology are described in Chapter 2.) Janice Morse (1999c) introduced the idea of methodological coherence through the heuristic of an armchair walkthrough, which has proven over and over again to be one of the most important learning tools for novice qualitative researchers. The armchair walkthrough is a process of thinking through the methodological trajectory of an entire research project. For instance, you might ask yourself: "If I ask *this* question, then I will need this or that kind of data, and to get that, I will have to interview these people or observe this or that" (Morse, 1999c, p. 435). In Table 1.1, I have provided an adaptation of the armchair walkthrough.

The important point with respect to Table 1.1 is to work horizontally. For example, you are interested in how some individuals are able to meet most of their needs with few material goods (nonconsumption).[3] Work on consumption, especially within the environmental literature, is burgeoning (Bauman, 2007; Princen, Maniates, & Conca, 2002). The thesis is simple: If we do not reduce consumption (from the use of natural resources by large industries to our personal take-out coffee cups), our environment will deteriorate (e.g., pollution, excessive demand of natural resources, global warming). Although consumption interests you, how people live with reduced consumption of material goods, in our consumption-driven society, intrigues you more. You have noticed that families with young children have a very high potential for consuming material goods. There is so much "stuff": baby joggers, exersaucers, outdoor toys for every season, video monitors, motorized SUVs, and innumerable toys. The line of *Baby Einstein* goods (so cleverly marketed) intimates that, if not purchased, our precious baby's emotional and physical health will be stunted and she or he will be relegated to a lifetime of failure.

Table 1.1: Armchair Walkthrough

| Ontology, Epistemology<br><br>Theoretical Position/ Perspective | Method | Research Question | Participants |
|---|---|---|---|
| Interpretivist/ Constructivist<br><br>Symbolic Interactionism | Grounded Theory | How do families come to practice and sustain non-consumption of material goods? | Parent with at least one child under the age of six self-identified as a non-consumer |
| Interpretivist<br><br>Existentialism Merleau-Ponty | Phenomenology | What is the lived experience of being a parent who practices non-consumption of material goods? | Parent with at least one child under the age of six self-identified as a non-consumer |
| | Ethnography | | |
| Poststructuralist | | | |
| Feminist | | | |
| Foucault | Discourse analysis | | |
| Narrative | | | |

You sit in your armchair and think through this topic. You want to ask the *question*: How do families come to practice and sustain non-consumption of material goods? This sounds like a grounded theory (*method*) research question, so you work within the first line of the chart. You will align yourself with the interpretivist tradition and constructivist perspective (*ontology* and *epistemology*) and will anchor the study in symbolic interactionism (*theoretical perspective*). Your *participants* are parents (regardless of age, ethnicity, etc.) with at least one child under the age of six who have identified themselves as nonconsumers of material

| Sample Size | Data Collection | Setting | Data Analysis | Results |
|---|---|---|---|---|
| 16-23 | Interviews | Place of participant's choice | Constant comparison | Model or substantive theory |
| 5-9 | Interviews Images | Place of participant's choice | Theming guided by four existentials | Rich description of the *essence* of the phenomenon |
| | | | | |
| | | | | |
| | | | | |
| | | | | |

goods. You just want to interview (*data collection*) one parent, a single parent, or if in a two parent family, the one who self-identifies as more reflective about the household consumption. You know that the *sample size* of a grounded theory is approximately twenty participants. You know that families who have reduced their consumption of material goods donate to and associate with certain groups in your city (e.g., environmental nongovernmental organizations, alternative food stores, and Earth Day festivals). This is where you will start recruitment and may do interviews in a quiet location anywhere the parent feels comfortable (*setting*). You will be using constant comparison for *data analysis*, and your *results* will be a model or substantive theory describing the process of coming to practice and sustaining nonconsumption of material goods.

However, on second thought this is not what you want to do. You stay in your armchair and think through the topic in a different way. You instead think what it means and feels like to "be" a parent who practices nonconsumption of material goods. You want to think about this through phenomenology (*method*) and so will "walk through" the second line of the chart. You are an interpretivist (*ontology* and *epistemology*), connect yourself with existentialism, have read a great deal of philosophy, and admire Maurice Merleau-Ponty's (2002) (*theoretical position/perspective*) work. Your *research question* might be: What is the lived experience of being a parent who practices nonconsumption of material goods? Your *participants* will still be one parent with at least one child under the age of six and you will recruit through the same agencies or groups listed above. You know that the *sample size* of a phenomenology is quite small, around eight participants. You will still interview (*data collection*) a parent at the location of their choice (*setting*). However, you want to include images (*data collection*) that demonstrate emotions and physical behaviors that are inferred from advertisements and art depicting consumption behavior (e.g., a young family in the sun, smiling and happy, playing with their children on their new jungle gym) or reduced or nonconsumption behavior (e.g., a mother cuddling with her baby, storytelling time). Your analytic technique will be theming through the four existentials: temporality (time), spatiality (space), corporeality (lived body) and relationality (human relation). More specifically, you want to draw on van Manen (1997), who has worked from Merleau-Ponty and Husserl, and his interactive aspects of inquiry and analysis. Your themes may be something like: "Satiation," "Gratitude," "Freedom," and "Meaning." Your *results* will be a rich, detailed description of the essence of the experience of being a nonconsumer.

Continuing on with the armchair walkthrough, you can decide what your study would look like if you took an ethnographic, poststructural-ist, feminist, discourse analysis, or narrative perspective, and so on. In other words, methodological coherence is following through (horizon-tally through Table 1.1) with a theoretical position/perspective and/or method and the attributes that constitute each method.

Notice that I used the expression *theoretical position/perspective and/or method*. Some researchers believe that theory and method are one and the same and that to discuss them separately is nonsensical. This is apparent, for example, by the two merged *theoretical position/perspec-tive and/or method* cells within the postmodern, feminist, and narrative trajectories. If working from these perspectives, you might not name a method. Others believe that a specific method must always be chosen or the research will be haphazard. In my experience, you can choose a theoretical position/perspective and not name a method. You can also choose a method and not name a particular theoretical position/perspec-tive. This is explained in more detail in Chapter 2.

The *armchair walkthrough* can help you design your study and main-tain methodological coherence. But what happens if your participants do not want to be interviewed or if they want to be interviewed but do not *want* to speak to the phenomenon (e.g., want to talk about how they decided to have children) or *cannot* articulate the phenomenon (e.g., can-not find words to describe non-consumption)? On the other hand, the local environmental organization staff, want to be interviewed about how they promote non-consumption, and you might want to avail yourself of this great opportunity. What happens then? You change your design where needed, move to another horizontal space within the table if nec-essary, and follow that flexible, but guided, route.

Back to the student who claimed to use phenomenology. This student is not thinking through her interest or question but is instead picking from all possible cells in the *armchair walkthrough* table. Although it is important to be able to change your data collection strategies, sam-pling, research question, method, and so on as the study-in-progress demands, you cannot just pick and choose from any possible qualitative strategy available, throw it into the soup, and expect it to work out. This makes qualitative work sloppy and unscientific. The result is "lousy" research, and the student will have nothing to report at the end of her study, other than how not to perform one.

I will refer to the principle of *methodological coherence* and the *arm-chair walkthrough* throughout this book. However, it is not my intention to make the contents of the cells in the armchair walkthrough prescriptive.

For example, phenomenologists analyze their data in many different ways, depending primarily on the philosopher they know best. The armchair walkthrough must be understood as a heuristic to help you plan your study and think through methodological coherence, not as what you *have* to do, for example, if you are doing a phenomenological study.

# Qualitative Annoyances

After teaching qualitative inquiry and talking with people about it over many years, I have a few minor irritations that can flare up into great frustration, particularly on bad days. I have mentioned one already, in the student discussed above, who wanted to do the very convoluted "postmodern, phenomenological" study; for such a student, the armchair walkthrough is helpful. I have a few other qualitative annoyances.

### "It's An Add-On"

Adding one or two open-ended questions at the conclusion of a survey or conducting a few interviews with people who filled out the survey does not make a study qualitative. The purpose of these few open-ended questions or interviews is to solicit comments. These add-ons do not require the iterative process of data collection, analysis, collection, analysis, and so forth, and are not substantive enough to yield any sort of stand-alone, publishable findings.

### "It Can Be Done by Journalists"

Journalists do not conduct qualitative inquiry. Students often ask me what the difference is between a good article in the local newspaper and qualitative research, as on the surface they seem quite similar. But there is a real distinction to be made. Journalists do hear/record a person's or people's stories and then write up the "data" into one story, which does resemble the qualitative research process. However, journalists do not have to know the literature; nor are they required to check, recheck, compare, contrast, and verify the data. They also do not have to sample purposefully and are not concerned with rigor. This does not mean that journalists do not do good and interesting work, but the journalists' job is to summarize comments to make a good story, not to do research.

## "It's Biased"

What about subjectivity and that bad, bad bias? When someone criticizes qualitative inquiry as biased or subjective, I laugh and thank them for the compliment. Bias can be understood in two ways. First, critics might say that the sample is biased and reject the research by thinking through all the problems caused by a biased sample. This criticism works from the principle of random sampling in quantitative inquiry where each member of the defined population has the chance of being included in the research sample. This principle enables generalization. For example, a student once asked, after hearing me comment that many of the women in the research and/or their partners had been jailed, how I was going to deal with my biased sample. In qualitative inquiry, there is no such thing as a biased sample. When a phenomenon is unknown (and a qualitative approach is necessitated), then we sample for the best examples of the phenomenon (Morse, 2006). We want to gather as much bias or a variety of experiences with the phenomenon so that we can describe it in its fullness. In other words, we deliberately seek out bias; participants' bias is exactly what we want to hear about.

Second, critics will say that qualitative inquiry is biased because it is fraught with what the researcher wants to see and say about the data, so the work is not neutral or objective. This is partially and, I am proud to say, true. I will discuss this more in the contexts of ontology, epistemology, and theoretical position/perspective in Chapter 2 and reflexivity in Chapter 10. I will also add that we have ways of managing this issue, which are addressed in the context of rigor in Chapter 7.

You should be aware, however, that no science, qualitative or quantitative, is neutral, objective, or value free. Absolute objectivity is impossible and even undesirable because of the social nature and human purposes of research. Written reports are always selective and reflect the stance, or orientation, of the writer. Instead of becoming mired in the terms *bias, subjective, objective,* and *neutral,* think about making your research rigorous regardless of whether it is qualitative or quantitative.

## "It's Not Empirical Research"

Some people think that *empirical* means experimental and shudder when it is used in conjunction with qualitative inquiry. I am not sure how empiricism developed into a synonym for experimentation, but it is a case of a definition gone awry. *Empirical* means observable through the senses. It is that which can be observed or experienced. Qualitative inquiry is empirical.

## "It's Only Anecdotal"

An anecdote is a story based on someone's personal life experience. Like any good story it tries to make a point, and over time the story is told over and over again. When people state that qualitative research is "only anec-dotal," they are often contrasting it with evidence. Anecdotes are stories, but stories within the context of qualitative research are data. Working with data thoughtfully, systematically, and theoretically is a scientific endeavor that produces knowledge and creates evidence. In other words, within the context of a qualitative research project, an anecdote does not exist.

## "It's Irrelevant"

Notions prevail that qualitative inquiry produces findings that are nei-ther generalizable nor applicable to clinical or community practice. If our research is not generalizable and irrelevant, why would we do it? The paradox, well stated by Sandelowski & Barroso (2003) "is that qualitative research is conducted in the 'real world'—that is, not in artificially con-trolled and/or manipulated conditions—yet is seen as not applicable to that world" (p. 784). There is more on this in Chapter 7 on Rigor.

# Summary

Welcome to qualitative inquiry. I am captivated by the endless oppor-tunities to ask and wonder about the human condition that qualitative inquiry provides. I hope the following chapters will intrigue you and provide you with a solid foundation for conducting a qualitative study. I must also advise you that this is just an introduction to a complex, broad, fascinating, and ever-evolving methodology.

## Exercise 1.1: Finding the Story behind the Numbers

The objective of this exercise is to demonstrate how qualitative inquiry and quantitative inquiry illuminate different aspects of an issue. This exercise can be conducted individually or in a small or large group.

Select an issue for which quantitative data (i.e., numbers) are available to help explain the issue. In one to two pages or in a class discussion, answer the following questions: What do these numbers tell you about the issue? What do the numbers *not* tell you about the issue? What is missing? What kind of information do you need to compliment your understanding of the issue? Construct a research question that would focus on hearing the stories behind the numbers.

## Chapter 2

# Theory and Method

In this chapter, I describe ontology, epistemology, and theoretical position/perspective and discuss how they collude to position or situate the researcher and provide a "lens" for conducting the research. I outline the difference between methodology and method and describe the relationship between theoretical position/perspective and method. I also address typical questions from researchers new to qualitative inquiry. These include: Can you do a feminist qualitative study? Or is feminism the "theoretical perspective" and you still need to choose a method, for example, a feminist grounded theory or a feminist ethnography?

I experience the divisions among qualitative researchers most acutely in my qualitative interdisciplinary graduate and postdoctoral seminar. I notice that important theories of students' disciplines—or those favored by their supervisors—have been read, have altered students' worldviews, and have become revered. They begin speaking of "Smith and Smith" or "this theory" and "that book." They talk their talk. The language of these theorists has power; it dazzles.

At first, students are astonished, but after a few seminars, other students admit that they have not read Smith and Smith, are unfamiliar with this or that, and think that the language of a revered theorist does not dazzle but only confuses. Some say forthrightly: "I am a critical theorist" or "I am third-wave feminist," whereas others let their eyes glaze over and say nothing at all. We all see "the problem" lying in the different research questions and we give more importance to some reearch questions than to others. These discussions often become personal. Even when I use the most carefully selected words, it is not about how my position/perspective or research question is different but how it is better.

Michael Agar (2004), in his keynote address "Know when to Hold 'Em, Know when to Fold 'Em: Qualitative Thinking outside the University," captured well the divides among qualitative researchers.

> As if we didn't have enough problems already. If qualitative researchers are contentious on how and when their methods can be used, they turn into tag-team wrestlers when asked to agree on a single definition for *qualitative*. We know anthropologists who sneer at the term, arguing that everything is already covered by *ethnography*. We know researchers who think the term labels a recipe, sort of a Chi-square, only with words instead of numbers. We know positivists who think of a Gutman scale as an exercise in qualitative slumming. And we know some qualitative researchers who battle to the death over the question of representation and others who couldn't give a damn, some who worship the puns that Derrida writes and others who think he's the researcher anti-Christ. (pp. 102–103)

Having to struggle continually with my own ever-changing place within these expansive divides, I have come to make some sense out of them for my own purposes and for students slogging through and sometimes slugging it out in seminars. To think through these divides requires more than answering the typical question of why you are interested in your topic or tacking a chapter on at the end of your dissertation about how you felt or how you changed because of your research. It is about ontology and epistemology and your theoretical position/perspective. These concepts are presented to assist the newcomer in getting through Agar's (2004) qualitative quandary.

## Ontology, Epistemology, and Theoretical Position/Perspective

In the late 1980s and into the 1990s, Guba and Lincoln (1994) outlined ontology and epistemology and how these concepts linked with research, making the discussion of these concepts possible. Spending time thinking through ontology and epistemology, as well as theoretical positions/perspectives, is time well spent. You can sort out most qualitative issues, including the most controversial ones, by being attuned to and always going back to your ontological, epistemological, and theoretical allegiances. Many students, however, feel discomfort when wading into these discussions, and rightly so. Some scholars give full attention to these issues, whereas others might only muse about them, and some do not attend to them at all. Moreover, even when we do attend to these issues, they tend to converge and coalesce, both in researchers' minds and in the literature, to make this discussion anything but straightforward.

But what about the *paradigm?* The research paradigm is the net that holds the researcher's ontology, epistemology, and theoretical position/perspective.[4] Thus, it consists of overarching, firmly held, conscious or unconscious, yet ever-changing convictions about what we can know about our world (ontology) and how we can know it (epistemology). More particularly, it includes how we position ourselves (theoretical position) or the perspective we take (theoretical perspective) within our world. It is a "basic set of beliefs that guides action" (Guba, 1990, p. 17).

The term *paradigm* captures all of these notions, but I do not think about paradigms when I work; they seem too broad to capture how strongly these notions can guide all aspects of my research. I like to think more specifically about ontology, epistemology, and theoretical position/perspective. When we consider these concepts, we are obliged to think about how we understand and appreciate research in general and our own research in particular, how we do it, and even how we write it up.

Briefly, ontology asks: What is the nature of reality? What can be known? (Guba & Lincoln, 1994). What can be apprehended? Following from ontology, epistemology asks: What is the relationship between the researcher and participant? Is it one of the knower and the known, or is it one of two knowing participants? (Gunzenhauser, 2006). It is essential that you figure out where you are situated ontologically and epistemologically. To do so, I ask you to think about the following.

We ask a research question, and through our research we provide the answer to it. While we conduct our research, the researcher and the participant (or other data sources) do not interact because while the interview questions are being asked, the researcher, maintaining objectivity, stands separate from the participant and asks a question, to which the participant responds. The answer to the research question is written with authority and becomes "truth" about how and why the phenomenon exists. There are no counters to this text. This description outlines a positivist perspective, which is embedded in a realist ontology (postpositivist in a critical realist ontology) and objective epistemology (Denzin & Lincoln, 2005).

On the other hand, we can think about research in another way. We ask a research question, and a conversation ensues. The researcher is attentive to how she interacts, shapes, and is shaped by the interaction and attests to this in some way in the text. Research is dialogic: It is about being in a relationship. It is, in the strongest and most powerful sense of the word, subjective. We assume that there are multiple realities and multiple truths and that we are presenting just one possibility. The resulting text is historically, culturally, and socially constructed. This generally describes a constructivist perspective rooted in a relativist ontology (multiple realities) and a subjectivist epistemology (researcher and participant co-create understanding) (Denzin & Lincoln, 2005).

There is yet another way to think about research that pushes the constructivist perspective a bit further. Not only are there multiple realities and multiple truths, but these realities and truths are structured by means or are a consequence of such factors as race, class, gender, age, and sexuality, among others (material-realist ontology) (Denzin & Lincoln, 2005). The researcher is in relation with the participant (or other data sources) (subjectivist epistemology) and not only accounts for it in the text but makes it explicit. A research text, in whatever form it may take, provides not the answer but many possibilities and, indeed, poses many questions.

These brief introductions to ontology and epistemology just skim the surface, so do not despair if you do not yet feel ready to legitimize yourself by naming your ontology and epistemology: Be patient and read on.

To refine, clarify, and lend words to describe your epistemological and ontological stance, you need to understand theoretical position/ perspective. I use *theoretical position/perspective* to encompass particular lenses, philosophers or philosophies, and theories or theoretical underpinnings that swirl above us and are referred to, inconsistently yet persistently, throughout qualitative writing. I choose the term *theoretical position/perspective* because I think it best describes the role that lenses, philosophies, and so on play in the research process. Theoretical positions/perspectives are ways that *theoretically* position the researcher in and with the world, meaning that they come from abstract (i.e., are not embedded in particular instances) notions, principles, or concepts of the world. In other words, the researcher can be positioned or take a perspective through a particular lens, philosopher, theory, or some sort of combination of all three.

When referring to theoretical position/perspective, I mean positions such as *critical theory, feminism(s), postcolonialism, postmodernism,* and *poststructuralism*. These positions/perspectives are overlapping, not mutually exclusive. They were originally articulated in response to positivism, which asserts that objectivity is possible and that objective statements on truths of the world can be made. Again, all authors hesitate when writing about these positions as there are many ways to understand and emphasize critical theory, feminism, and so on. This means that critical theory(s), feminism(s), and so on actually exist. In this spirit, I will now outline the more widely cited positions.

*Critical theory* is often considered an umbrella term that encompasses or has evolved into further theoretical positions/perspectives, such as feminism, postcolonialism, postmodernism, and poststructuralism. *Critical theory* focuses on unequal relations of power and, according to Kincheloe and McLaren (2005), assumes that:

   a) all thought is mediated by socially and historically constructed power relations;

   b) facts are embedded in dominant values and ideology;

   c) language is crucial to the development of subjectivity;

   d) certain groups are privileged over others and that oppression holds firm when those oppressed "accept their social status as natural, necessary, or inevitable";

   e) oppression comes in many forms (e.g., classism, racism, sexism, ageism) and cannot be considered separately and;

   f) dominant research practices often, although unintentionally, reproduce "systems of class, race, and gender oppression." (p. 304)

Thus, as critical theorists you will attempt to use your work "as a form of social or cultural criticism" (p. 304).

Using these underlying assumptions from critical theory, we can say that if you claim a *feminist* position/perspective, you will work from the assumption that the nature of reality "is unequal and hierarchical" (Skeggs, 1994, p. 77) and will conceptualize the study, collect, and analyze the data, and explain the findings through a gendered perspective. Your goal will be to reveal, in some way, social position and gender inequity of women. Working from a *postcolonial* position/perspective, you will challenge the dominant discourse and intrinsic assumptions and bring to light the material and discursive corollaries of colonialism (Crush, 1994).

A *postmodern* position/perspective rejects the modernist or enlightenment period, which claims a purely rational route to knowledge and progress through positivist science. As a postmodernist, you would not privilege any theory, method, or tradition, and so on as the only way or form of knowledge (Richardson & St. Pierre, 2005). You question all methods as to how they serve particular interests. You understand how knowledge is politically, historically, and culturally created, so, although research from a postmodern perspective produces a limited and local knowledge, it is still knowledge that can reveal and inform.

As a poststructuralist, you focus on language and link it with "subjectivity, social organization, and power" (Richardson & St. Pierre, 2005, p. 961). Language produces meaning and creates social reality, thus dividing and socially organizing the world. Language creates centers of power through which one's sense of self—one's subjectivity—is constructed (Richardson & St. Pierre, 2005), so what something means to someone exists through available discourses. For example, if you are the executive director of a nonprofit community organization operating primarily through funders' guidelines and discourses, you might think about "serving clients," "case management," "outcomes and deliverables," and "closing the file " after their "needs" are met. Work will be structured and performed through these discourses. Yet people are not "cases to be managed."

Some researchers who take on critical or "post" positions/perspectives describe themselves as being positioned through such theories such as queer, Marxist, critical race or ethnic theory, or symbolic interactionism, to name a few. It is important, however, to understand that *theory* in this sense is not a substantive theory such as attachment theory or stress and coping theory. These substantive theories deal with a particular content area or field of inquiry (e.g., parent-child relations as explained through attachment theory or living with HIV/AIDS as explained through stress and coping theory). Theory, referring to theoretical position/perspective, is more general and conceptually abstract and is based on notions, principles, or concepts of why and how the world works as it does.

Although some researchers align themselves with a particular theoretical position; others prefer to attach their work to a particular philosopher. Such philosophers include Bourdieu, Deleuze, Derrida, Foucault, Lyotard, Heidegger, and Husserl. Researchers make explicit the tenets of the philosopher through whom they are working, many specifically "fathers" of particular positions (e.g., Derrida and poststructuralism) to frame their research. For example, philosophers such as Heidegger and Husserl, as well as Merleau-Ponty, Gadamer, Wittgenstein, and so on primarily guide the work of phenomenologists.

The short list and brief descriptions of these positions/perspectives that I have provided here are meant not to be exhaustive. I have included them to enable you to appreciate how strongly such positions can guide all aspects of your research.

We now return to the seminar, where some students are troubled by the entire discussion about ontology, epistemology, and theoretical position/perspective. I remind them that adhering to a particular theoretical position/perspective does not mean that they can count on agreement among those researchers who claim this same position/perspective. Although common threads exist, the evolving nature and interpretation of each means that it is more correct to speak of feminism(s) or postmodernism(s), for example, or varying understandings of Merleau-Ponty's work than to believe in an absolute of each. As I have truly struggled to comprehend some of these main theoretical positions/perspectives and philosophers' work, I felt relieved when I read an interview with Michel Foucault (1998), a venerated French philosopher and historian, in which he so honestly and unabashedly asked, "What are we calling post-modernity? I'm not up to date" (p. 447).

How do you get through this qualitative quagmire? You must read and read about philosophy and theoretical positions/perspectives and, equally important, speak with fellow students and colleagues about these challenging works and ideas. If you spend time with these issues, even if you cannot name your epistemology in one or two words or give a label to your theoretical position/perspective (e.g., "I am a feminist"), you will be able to handle the epistemology, position/perspective, or any other of these types of questions very well. The most important thing is this: Do not be lured into claiming falsely to "be" something, pigeonholing yourself into a particular theoretical position/perspective. To do research, you do not need a title for yourself; you need to be able to think for yourself.

So, do you, as Agar (2004) stated, "worship the puns that Derrida writes," or do you "think he's the researcher anti-Christ" (p. 103)? Your answer is not a life sentence. As you grow through your research career, you will take on and push aside different perspectives, and some will stay with you your whole life. You will become more adventurous in your approaches yet will still appreciate more traditional studies that are well done and illuminating.

Once you are comfortable with your epistemological, ontological, and theoretical position/perspective, it is time to choose a method. Or is it?

# Methodology and Method

We do an exercise (see Exercise 2.1) in class called Sorting It Out. The purpose of this exercise is to "sort out" ontology, epistemology, theoretical position/perspective, method, data collection strategy, data analysis strategy, and results. It begins with having students name any qualitative *method* they have heard of or are familiar with. Students suggest numerous terms, some of which I have never heard of and some I know well. The very well-established ones are usually named first: ethnography, grounded theory, and phenomenology. Then I hear participatory action research, discourse analysis, narrative, and visual methods. Ethnoscience and institutional ethnography are sometimes put on the list.

Theoretical positions/perspectives, such as feminism(s) and Foucault, always get mixed in. Interviews and focus groups are also mentioned regularly. Sometimes terms such as "soft," "anecdotal," and "generalizabilty" are mentioned; they do not make it into the chart, but become an opportunity to discuss what these terms are and why they do not fit into the chart. I map out the students' answers under one or more of the headings found in Table 2.1. For instance, feminism(s) goes into the Theoretical Position/Perspective column, participatory action research goes into the Method column, and focus groups go into the Data Collection Strategy column. Our list gets more dubious as the exercise continues, and laughter ensues as I am stumped over what to do with some of the methods named. In fact, I do not know how to pronounce or even spell some of them. See Table 2.1 for a typical example of the Sorting It Out exercise and Exercise 2.1 if you would like to work through this process. It is important to read Table 2.1 by column (not row).

The point of this exercise is to help identify what is ontology, epistemology, theoretical position, perspective, a method, a data collection strategy, a data analysis strategy and results, and what is not. For instance, it is amazing how many students, when asked, "What method are you using?" answer, "Interviews." Interviews, focus groups, participant observation, videos, and still images are examples of data collection strategies; they are not theoretical positions/perspectives and/or methods. Data collection strategies do not assume a theoretical direction; nor do they provide an overall set of strategies and procedures that guide inquiry. They are ways to collect data. When asked what theoretical position/perspective and/or method you are working from, please do not reply, "Focus groups."

Table 2.1: Sorting It Out

| Ontology, Epistemology Theoretical Positions | Methods | Data Collection Strategies | Data Analysis Strategies | Results |
|---|---|---|---|---|
| Feminism | Ethnography | Interviews | Constant comparison | Theory |
| Foucault | Grounded theory | Focus groups | Theming | Matrix |
| Critical theory | Phenomenology | Participant observation | Content analysis | Taxonomy |
| Critical race theory | Participatory action research | Photographs | | Story |
| Postcolonialism | Discourse analysis | Video | | Collage |
| Postmodernism | Narrative | | | Film |
| Poststructuralism | Visual methods | | | Drama |
| Bourdieu | Ethnoscience | | | Description |
| Deleuze | Institutional ethnography | | | |
| Derrida | Visual ethnography | | | |
| Foucault | | | | |
| Heidegger | | | | |
| Husserl | | | | |

The next step is to tackle the differences first between methodology and method and then between theory and method. Methodology and method are areas where researchers often assume that they are using the same working definitions but quickly find out that these terms mean different things to different people. *Methodology* is, simply, the study of methods. The use of the term, however, has become a bit complicated within the discussion of ontology and epistemology and includes the ways we gain knowledge about the world including experimental, manipulative, dialogical, or dialectical approaches (Guba & Lincoln, 1994). Methodology thus entails theoretical positions and perspectives and involves thinking through method, data collection strategies, analysis techniques, and the production and presentation of findings. It "involves theorizing about how we find things out; it is about the relationship between the process and the product of research" (Letherby, 2003, p. 5). It is "a theory and analysis of how research does or should proceed" (Harding, 1987, p. 3).

Method exists within methodology. A *method* "is a collection of research strategies and techniques based on theoretical assumptions that combine to form a particular approach to data and mode of analysis" (Richards & Morse, 2007, p. 2). In other words, a method provides a set of procedures, not prescriptions, that outline, for instance, the method's data collection strategies, typical sample size, and analytical strategies. Common methods include grounded theory, ethnography, and phenomenology.

All methods demand their own ways of thinking, working with the data, and writing or (re)presenting participants. Following the method's procedures ensures methodological coherence (see Chapter 1). If you are working within ethnography, you must think like an ethnographer. If you are working within phenomenology, you must think like a phenomenologist. Choosing a method involves a choice about how the researcher best believes the phenomenon can be revealed, problematized, or described. Simply put, it is how best to answer the research question.

However, similar questions about theoretical position/perspective apply to method: Do I have to "be" something (e.g., a grounded theorist)? Do I have to claim a method? What if my study does not fit into a particular method? My answer is the same: Do not falsely pigeonhole yourself into or claim hollow faithfulness to a particular method if you do not find this useful.

## Relationship between Theoretical Position/Perspective and Method

A sociologist may do a feminist qualitative study but not name a method. A nurse may do a grounded theory study but not name a theoretical position/perspective. Is there something *wrong* with this? Not necessarily.

Theoretical position/perspective and method: Herein lies the problem. Some researchers believe that theory and method are one and the same and that to discuss them separately is nonsensical. Others believe that a specific method must always be chosen or the research will be haphazard. My place is in the middle, and I have certainly not chosen this middle path to make it easier on me or on those I work with. I suggest that you can choose a theoretical position/perspective and not name a method. You can also choose a method and not name a particular theoretical position/perspective. Alternatively, you can choose to name a theoretical position/perspective *and* a method. Like the sociologist in the previous paragraph, you can do a feminist qualitative study. Like the nurse, you can do a grounded theory. You can also do a feminist grounded theory. You can take a postcolonial approach and produce a superior study. You can take a postcolonial, feminist, ethnographic approach and have a superior study. As long as these positions/perspectives and methods make sense together (i.e., methodological coherence), you can proceed sensibly. However, it is highly unlikely that a poststructuralist grounded theory would be attempted. This theoretical position/perspective and that method do not align well. This means that you do not necessarily have to name a method when you are working from strong theoretical positions/perspectives. Rather, the tenets of the theoretical position/ perspective guide the work.

To sit in this middle place, where theoretical position/perspective and method both matter, you must be comfortable with a wide range of possibilities and research questions. Method is important, yet we cannot become so preoccupied with it that we disregard ontology, epistemology, theoretical positions/perspectives, or the ideas of great thinkers, which direct us and our research in more profound ways than we can ever fully know. Similarly, theoretical position is important, but not to the point where we can dismiss well-established methods with their accompanying strategies, procedures, and protocols. Regardless, what is fundamental is making thoughtful, wise decisions through the course of the research so that at the end you will have something to conclude or "problematize" about the data you collected.

In my classroom lecture on theoretical position/perspective and method, I ask students to read a transcript from a study that I conducted on cultural competence in hospitals. I then ask them to begin coding it. Many of our "findings" are similar, but some diverge. Some students focus on the language and clearly see racist language in participants' accounts (i.e., discourse analysis). Some see how the culture of the hospital supports certain behaviors of the participants (i.e., ethnography). Some find remnants of colonialism and see categories developing along the lines of the adage "When in Rome, do as the Romans" (i.e., postcolonialism). Some want to detail the process of how cultural competence is carried out in hospitals (i.e., grounded theory). In other words, some students immediately think through theoretical positions/perspectives, but others do so through methods. And neither group is *wrong*.

# Summary

In my interdisciplinary experience, choosing between theory and method, or treating them as distinct, or touting one as better than the others is absurd and says more about how disciplines discipline themselves than it does about qualitative inquiry. Outlining the interplay between these concepts, as well as the ontology, epistemology, theoretical position/perspective, and method, enables the qualitative newcomer a path through the somewhat unclear and convoluted qualitative literature in this area. Once these concepts begin to make sense, you can move into the unbounded and uneven terrain of methods.

## Exercise 2.1: Sorting It Out

The objective of this exercise is to identify terms associated with ontology, epistemology, theoretical position/perspective, method, data collection strategies, data analysis strategies, and results. Doing so assists in organizing the methods section of your proposal, manuscript, and/or thesis. This works both in a large group or small group setting.

In a large or small group, take Table 2.1 as it appears in this chapter or, preferably, start anew and write out the column headings only. If you begin with Table 2.1., discuss whether you agree with the terms listed in each column, and why or why not. Move terms around if necessary. The next step is to name other terms that do not appear in the table, decide where to place them, and discuss why.

Alternately, if you begin with column headings only, start a free-flow list of any terms associated with qualitative inquiry and try to sort according to the headings. Make sure to keep a list of terms named, but not fitting for the table, and discuss the place of these terms in qualitative inquiry. Note the areas of disagreement and try to determine why members hold opposing conceptions of the term.

# Chapter 3

## Method

This chapter describes a range of qualitative methods, from those that consider the researcher as explicitly inherent in the research (e.g., autoethnography), through to more traditional methods (e.g., phenomenology, ethnography, and grounded theory), and includes newer methods that have grown out of the traditional methods (e.g., participatory action research, institutional ethnography).

I love theory; I enjoy methods. I enjoy sitting with a student and considering all the possible ways to explore his or her topic. I like research design and working through a process, but, better yet, I look forward to having that design challenged and modified as I interface with images and/or participants and their ideas. I enjoy thinking through what we are doing and how we are doing it as much as, or more than, releasing the findings. I love the social aspect of research and know that doing any kind of qualitative research, involving any method, is a commitment to a relation of some sort. That is why I study research methods.

Philosophers and scholars have contributed over centuries, building on each other's thoughts and theories to create and modify each of the methods that are outlined in this chapter. I will present a brief description of each method as an introduction to provide the newcomer to qualitative inquiry with some of the chutzpah required to get through the initial immersion in the field.

# Choosing a Method

The question of how to choose a research method has one customary and very good answer: You choose a method based on your research question. Simply, how does the research question demand to be treated? Beyond this, other reasons exist for choosing a method that the innocent and unsuspecting newcomer to research must appreciate. First, there is the reality that, regardless of the phenomenon, we tend to ask similar questions based on how we like to engage with and explain the world. Ethnographers, grounded theorists, phenomenologists, and discourse analysts, for example, can observe the same phenomenon but will naturally ask different questions of it.

Four qualitative researchers walk into their favorite coffee shop on a cold morning and become intrigued with studying its customers and the setting. The *ethnographer* will ask: "What is coffee shop culture?" He or she will look for symbols (e.g., coffee cup designs), patterns, and norms of behavior, and particulars of language that help us understand coffee shop behavior. The ethnographer might try to distinguish between the "to stay" and the "to go" customers or the "latte" and the "regular" customers. He or she asks these questions to reveal the intricacies and explain the behavior of others in certain social settings, to make their behavior comprehensible to others. The *grounded theorist* might examine how ordering the coffee occurs, from the moment people enter the shop to when they leave it, including how choices are made, if and how people chat in line, and the task of paying. The basic social process might be about "waiting for coffee." She or he always seems to be asking questions about process: how and why things happen, or how people go through an experience. A *phenomenologist*, on the other hand, might try to capture the essence of the first taste. Descriptions might include the feeling in the body: the smell, how taste buds "wake up," how the heart starts pounding. This researcher feels compelled to study, in depth, the first taste of coffee so that a non–coffee drinker can understand what that experience is like. The *discourse analyst* would focus particularly on the language and likely look for the power embedded in more elite or obscure coffee language—"I'll have an el grande, decaf mochachino, no fat, no foam"—versus the more plain language ("I'll have a regular coffee"). She or he will most definitely be intrigued by the sign hanging in the window of the coffee shop: "We don't speak French, Spanish or Starbucks." We often tend toward different methods because of how we naturally ask questions of the world.

Second, there is also the very practical reality that if you have immersed yourself in the writings of Gadamer for three years, you will be inclined to undertake hermeneutical phenomenology. If you have studied the history and maturation of grounded theory since its origins in 1967, you will likely conduct a grounded theory, and if you have studied poststructural theory and have found yourself the only one teaching the course in the department, you will probably situate and conduct your research as a poststructuralist.

Third, certain schools, departments, and faculties espouse certain methods. You might hear, for example, "This school does grounded theory." Be aware of this when choosing your graduate school: If you do not feel comfortable with grounded theory but all of the research and theses coming out of the school are grounded theory, you might want to relocate.

With all of these reasons for choosing a method, keep in mind that it is your goal to become a competent researcher, able to discuss, in depth, a variety of theories and methods. Be open to new branches and maturations of theories and methods, and, above all, use common sense to think through the research process.

## The Methods

For the purposes of learning, the methods discussed below are introduced as distinct from each other, but, as stated above, their histories intersect, and aspects of each have been used to build and modify each method over time. In addition, it is impossible to provide a description of every method proposed in qualitative inquiry. If a student or colleague has thought seriously about using a given method in the past five years, I have included it. This does not mean that others are less valuable, however, and I encourage you to go beyond the ones described here if none of them makes sense for you. As well, it is possible that someone you know or have worked with has done excellent, "legitimate" qualitative research for which there is as yet no name (Morse, 1991a). Finally, remember that choosing a method might not be necessary; a researcher may be guided by the tenets of a theoretical position/perspective (e.g., feminism, postmodernism, poststructuralism) throughout the research process. For a reminder of the armchair walkthrough, see Table 1.1 (Chapter 1).

I begin this section with a description of traditional ethnography, followed by adaptations to the ethnographic method that, although rooted in traditional ethnography, have become stand-alone ways of approaching a research question: focused ethnography, critical and feminist ethnography, institutional ethnography, autoethnography, ethnoscience, participatory action research, photovoice, photonovella, and community mapping. Other methods include grounded theory, situational analysis, phenomenology, narrative, case study, discourse analysis, conversational analysis, interpretive description, descriptive qualitative, concept analysis, semiotics, and collective biography. I have also included a comment on mixed method. Following a brief description of each method, I provide the title of a research article or book that uses the particular method by way of example. Exercise 3.1 (Many Methods and the Armchair Walkthrough) is an opportunity to apply each method to an area of interest to note the similarities and differences among, as well as the results following from, each method.

## Ethnography

Ethnography, with its foundations in late 19th-century anthropology, is considered one of the oldest qualitative methods. With their discipline "grounded in a commitment to the firsthand experience and exploration of a particular social or cultural setting on the basis of (though not exclusively by) participant observation" (Atkinson et al., 2001, p. 4), ethnographers have traditionally sought to understand cultures other than their own, especially those most exotic, alluring, or unfamiliar. They enter the field with their attention focused by generations of anthropological theory (e.g., structure that creates order, ritual that is part of identity, meaning of symbols). Although ethnography has changed considerably since the late 19th century, many of the basic principles underlying the method remain.

Working within the concept of culture (e.g., beliefs, values, behaviors, norms, symbols, artifacts, language) of a group of people, traditional ethnographers join a group's setting to learn about its way of life. A focus can be on the language of the group and how it develops and gives clues to what is going on in the culture. When describing traditional ethnography, I refer to Margaret Mead (adviser Franz Boas) and her study *Coming of Age in Samoa* (Mead, 1928/2001), examining the adolescence experience in Papua New Guinea.

However, we no longer believe that we need to travel to far-away places to study culture; nor is culture defined only along ethnic or geographical lines. We understand that cultures and subcultures are everywhere and are found among people in a specific place (e.g., a faculty, hospital, or community-serving organization) or among people who share a similar experience but might not know each other (e.g., street kids, graduate students, parents who have adopted, or military personnel). Ethnographers use participant observation (field notes), interviews, and documents to collect their data. This is not data triangulation, however; these three data collection strategies define traditional ethnography. Other data sources include cultural artifacts, video, poetry, and art, among others. Ethnographers usually conduct a content analysis on their data (See Chapter 6).

The end result of ethnography is an attempt to describe the culture of a given group as the individuals in the group see it. This is the *emic* (as opposed to *etic*) view: how individuals within a culture (not outside observers) describe and construct meaning about cultural norms and behavior. As Spradley (1979) said: "I want to understand the world from your point of view. I want to know what you know in the way you know it. I want to understand the meaning of your experience, to walk in your shoes, to feel things as you feel them, to explain things as you explain them. Will you become my teacher and help me understand? (p. 34).

An ethnography might appear as a thick description of a group's social or cultural setting or as a taxonomy or framework to name objects and their relations. The goal in traditional ethnography is to make the culture intelligible and comprehensible to others. Because the purpose of traditional ethnography is to describe the culture, the goal is not to critique, judge, or design action plans to bring about change within the culture.

I will add a cautionary note, however. As mentioned previously, ethnography is embedded in the concept of culture, which is problematic in our postmodern world, linked as it is to colonialism, essentialism, typologies, generalizations, labels, and on and on: how we describe, define, and finalize people through a cultural account. Michael Agar (2006) valiantly took on the concept in an article, which I recommend that you read to help you struggle with this concept. Regardless of how you come through the culture debate, do not let this discourage your interest in ethnography and culture, whatever that may be. My advice is to be aware of the debate and then proceed wisely.

Tourigny (1998) told the story of African American young people in inner-city Detroit deliberately seeking HIV exposure. What seems implausible and preposterous behavior is made intelligible to me through this ethnography. After reading it, I understand why these young people, with "feelings of hopelessness and futility … within the context of marginalization, insensitive social policies, and demanding caretaking responsibilities," welcome HIV/AIDS (p. 149).

## Focused Ethnography

Focused ethnography is a more targeted form of ethnography and is led by a specific research question, conducted within a particular context or organization among a small group of people to inform decision-making regarding a distinct problem. Compared to traditional ethnography, it is more time limited. Participant observation is often conducted at particular times or events, or not at all. Focus groups can be conducted along with or instead of interviews, and participants might not know each other but come together under the same experience (e.g., a cancer support group) (Richards & Morse, 2007). As in traditional ethnography, an analytic technique is often content analysis.

In one focused ethnography, the authors explored new mothers' "responses to care given by male nursing students during and after birth" (Morn et al., 1999, p. 83). New mothers had definite thoughts about what was appropriate care for a male nurse to provide (e.g., not perineal care) and why, described through both personal (e.g., embarrassment) and contextual (e.g., characteristics of male student) factors. This focused ethnography was important for determining how to offer the best educative experience for male nursing students while providing patients with optimal nursing care.

## Critical and Feminist Ethnography

Critical ethnography and feminist ethnography are examples of a theoretical position being specifically named and combined with a method. If you think through the tenets of critical theory and ethnography or of feminist theory and ethnography, you will arrive at critical ethnography and feminist ethnography, respectively.

Critical ethnography has been described as traditional ethnography with a political agenda. Thomas (1993) has depicted it as analyzing and opening "to scrutiny otherwise hidden agendas, power centers, and assumptions that inhibit, repress, and constrain" (pp. 2–3). It promotes and encourages questioning of taken-for-granted assumptions. Critical ethnography requires us to link participants' experiences to broader structures of social power and control and explain how these structures reinforce existing social images of our participants. The method compels us to ask: "Why should we be content to understand the world instead of trying to change it?" (Marx, 1846/1974, in Thomas, 1993, p. 2).

Thomas's (1993) critical ethnography in prisons makes the behavior and norms of the prison culture, the intentions of inmates, and prison violence comprehensible to the reader. Rather than interpreting prison violence as barbaric and condemning the inmates for their behavior, he makes apparent the motivations of inmates and the function of violence in the prison culture.

Feminist ethnography, a form of critical ethnography, reveals the social inequalities between genders that are inherent in the culture or social setting under study. Feminist ethnographers, by linking women's experiences to broader structures of social power and control, explain how these structures reinforce existing social images of women.

Although not labeled as such, *Troubling the Angels* (Lather & Smithies, 1997) can be considered a feminist ethnography as it "explores the cultural meanings and social ramifications" (p. xiii) of women living with HIV/AIDS. As a reader, I understand how these women try to make sense of what is happening to them and what they make happen for themselves. The analysis extends to each of us to think about "meeting what we cannot know: death and the future" and how we make these things "present in the way we live our lives" (p. xiii). The book is also a good example of a layered text, a form of experimental writing.

## Institutional Ethnography

As in other critical theoretical approaches or methods, in institutional ethnography (IE) the researcher examines the role of knowledge and power in our everyday lives and how it shapes what we say and do. Based on the work of sociologist and feminist scholar Dorothy Smith in particular, IE enables the researcher to examine organizational text and language as a form of power and to address how this externally organized text, in turn, organizes social relations (Campbell & Gregor, 2002). Once an individual can see the power in institutional/organizational text, how institutions dominate and subordinate, reward and punish, through their text, and how he or she fits into this socially—deliberately and systematically—organized system, he or she can plan how to counter this domination (Campbell & Gregor, 2002). IE provides the opportunity to "map" out how and why things happen as they do (Campbell & Gregor, 2002). By engaging and theorizing about organizational texts, researchers become critics of the legitimized texts while also seeing how they, too, participate in and actively constitute and are constituted by these texts.

An IE was conducted to determine what happened to a ten-year-old child with Rett syndrome who, according to a coroner's report, died of severe malnutrition but who was determined to be "dying from a terminal illness," according to assessments conducted by an emergency physician, a hospice volunteer, and a home care nurse (Bell & Campbell, 2003, p. 113). The authors of this study outlined how these professional/ organizational texts colluded to construct the girl to be "dying of a terminal illness," and how this led to a do-not-resuscitate order. The authors demonstrate how the authority underlying text displaces "other forms of knowing in health care" (p. 113).

## Autoethnography

Between 1972 and 1984, Carolyn Ellis conducted an ethnography for her graduate research, comparing two isolated fishing communities. During that time, she lived the disjunction between the way she had been taught to conduct her research—"observe from a distance, keep myself out of the story and even my line of vision, and dispassionately record what I saw and heard" (Ellis, 2004, p. 9)—and how she actually engaged with the community. On the heels of this experience, her brother and her partner both died, pushing her to explore what to do with the intense emotion she experienced. She believed that writing her story would help others understand their experiences sociologically. Ellis's *story*, quite appropriately, tells how the method of autoethnography gained scientific grounding and popularity.

Autoethnography is a self-narrative that connects the personal to the cultural by placing understanding of self within a social context (Reed-Danahay, 1997). Autoethnographies "are highly personalized accounts that draw upon the experience of the author/researcher for the purposes of extending sociological understanding" (Sparkes, 2000, p. 21). This method has been criticized in the literature as self-indulgent and narcissist, and certainly not research. It has been argued, however, that because autoethnography connects "the personal to the cultural" (Ellis & Bochner, 2000, p. 739), enabling one to focus outward on the sociocultural aspects of one's experiences, it is research.

When I present autoethnography to students, many ask about the difference between autoethnography and other methods, such as personal narratives, self-ethnography, interpretive biography, or socioautobiography, to name a few. Ellis and Bochner (2000) have greatly helped out with this persistent question, noting that the term *autoethnography* has been around for at least two decades and that it can encompass those studies that have been referred to by terms such as the ones above. They provide an extensive list of terms that they include under the rubric of autoethnography.

The autoethnography of Andrew Sparkes (1996), whose "fatal flaw" in the form of a chronic lower back problem terminated his involvement in a top-class competitive sport, tells his story within what Western culture has taught us about "gender, age, ableness, social class, race, ethnicity, and sexuality" (p. 487). Sarah Wall (2006) wrote an autoethnography about learning about autoethnography that might be helpful to those who, as she states, might be "warming up to this method" (p. 3).

## Ethnoscience

Ethnoscience is a unique linguistic method of obtaining cultural knowledge from what people say (Leininger, 1985). It is about gaining insight into how people think and make decisions based on the assumption that thought, with all its cultural influences, is embedded in language. The ethnoscientist orders and categorizes data collection through interviews into domains, segregates, and subsegregates to make apparent the relationships within and among linguistic terms (Leininger, 1985). In turn, the ordering of terms helps the researcher learn how individuals order and experience their world.

Olson, Krawchuk, and Quddusi (2007) conducted a study using ethnoscience in which they interviewed participants with advanced cancer (i.e., currently receiving active treatment or palliative care), their family members or friends, and nurses who had cared for them to understand cancer patients' experiences with tiredness, fatigue, and/or exhaustion. The three domains (tiredness, fatigue, and exhaustion) were characterized by the same segregates (*emotions, thinking, muscles, how the body feels,* and *interactions with others*), but the subsegregates were different. These results were used to support their assertion that tiredness, fatigue, and exhaustion are, indeed, different concepts; the results led to the development of a fatigue adaptation model.

## Participatory Action Research

Participatory action research (PAR) grew out of the empowerment, liberation, and consciousness-raising works of Paulo Freire in the 1970s. It is based on the notion that "people have a universal right to participate in the production of knowledge which is a disciplined process of personal and social transformation" (Freire, 1997, p. xi). PAR entered the Western research world at a time of increasing distrust of traditional research via researchers with an unapologetic political and social justice agenda of empowering community members to take action over their circumstances and address their communities' issues. Indeed, in PAR the community group has ownership over the entire research process. Individuals and communities are no longer "subjects" or "objects" of research but are considered experts of their own experience, with complementary knowledge and skills to contribute to the research process.

In its earlier conceptualization, PAR was considered as such only if community people were involved in every stage of the research, from identification of the research problem, design of the study, data collection and analysis, and interpretation of the findings through to dissemination of the results. In addition, PAR focused at first on skill building among community members and capacity building within the community. Now the difficulties of doing PAR, given the structures of academia (ethics boards, publication demands, ownership of data, etc.) and constraints within particular research settings (e.g., institutions such as hospitals, schools, or group homes), make adhering to PAR in its entirety very difficult and, in some cases, undesirable. PAR has, accordingly, shifted to enabling community members to determine when and in what ways they would like to be involved in the research. Regardless of whether it is more traditional or an adapted version of PAR, the PAR process of engaging community members in *what is* (the needs, resources, and constraints within their present community) and *what could be* (the community they envision) is considered a consciousness-raising, health-promoting activity in itself and of equal importance to the research outcome.

Other methods that get mixed in with PAR include action research (AR), collaborative inquiry, appreciative inquiry, popular education, participatory research (PR), community-based participatory research, community-based collaborative research, community-participatory partnered research, and community-directed research, to name a few.

Although the differences among these approaches/methods are not at all clear in the literature, the differentiation between AR and PAR is among the questions most frequently asked by graduate students. Simply put, AR is PR without the political agenda. According to Stoecker (2004), it emphasizes "the integration of theory and practice," but "does not challenge the existing power relationships in either knowledge or material production" (p. 4).

In a book edited by Smith, Willms, and Johnson (1997), PAR is introduced in the context of six international health case studies in Mexico, Canada, India, Uganda, Chile, and Honduras. For example, one case describes the work of a Canadian dairy farmer and a Mexican educator and community activist in a Mexican *campesino* (farmer) cooperative and how their project was transformed from an act of charity to one of solidarity (Debbink & Ornelas, 1997).

## Photovoice and Photonovella

Photovoice and photonovella "are related approaches for participant-driven photo-based research" (Emme, in press). Photovoice blends a participatory approach with photography and social action by giving cameras to people to photograph their everyday lives and concerns. Through photography, participants act as recorders of their own experience and are in control of how they represent themselves and their lives. The assumption in photovoice is that images are powerful: They can teach and communicate needs, concerns, and stories in ways unavailable through written text. Photos elicit questions such as: "Why does this situation exist? Do we want to change it, and if so, how?" (Wang et al., 2004, p. 911). Essential to photovoice is the involvement of policymakers, other decision makers, media, funders, and others in the project who might, through the discussion of the photos, instigate change.

One of the first photovoice articles published involved Chinese village women (see Wang, Burris, & Ping, 1996) taking photos of their everyday lifework burdens as farmers engaged in long days of heavy farm labor. Photographs of babies in tobacco and cornfields, exposed to sun and heavy rain, as well as unsupervised older children, led to the establishment of a day care program. Images showing the lack of birth support and the widespread use of unsterilized instruments such as scissors helped bring about a midwifery program. Photographs of rural girls taking care of younger siblings during school hours drew attention to the

FIGURE 3.1: PHOTO ENTITLED "TRAFFIC LAWS"

lack of importance placed on girls' education and provided the impetus for a scholarship program. In a photovoice project that I am currently working on, we examine the experience of accessing health and social services by women with low income. The photograph shown in Figure 3.1 was taken by one participant, who provided the following description.

> I took this picture because they're putting too many tickets—there's too many traffic laws and people can't remember all of them. They're charging so much for all these tickets and fines, they're making so much money off them, but where's the money going? Drivers can't go anywhere, people are breaking laws all the time. It's getting ridiculous because some of these places are confusing to the drivers, they don't understand how the signs are, how the roads are. We don't know which way to go, which road to drive, the right way, the wrong way... there're too many signs and too many detours. And now I heard they have yellow light cameras. But sometimes you have to go through yellow lights. Like sometimes in winter time, if the roads are icy, I cannot stop. But if I go through that yellow light, it's automatically my fault. It's not my fault the roads are icy. What can you do? If you can't stop you can't stop. Like it's about the government, there's way too much regulation overall. This is a big country, a big city, people need to drive. There're a lot of drivers

here. But they don't pay attention to the real problems. They have so much time to make all these laws. Somebody is sitting there and saying let's make this law, let's make this law. Why are they not having someone sit there to make laws for the bigger problems?

A deeper analysis of this photo by the photovoice participants led to a discussion about how these mothers see government intervention infiltrating their entire lives. Yellow-light cameras become unreasonable when you have had numerous and long-term involvement with social services and child welfare, and the government continues to neglect the larger issue; namely, poverty.

Photonovella (or fotonovela) is the creation of "narratives built around sequential images" (Emme, in press). It begins with participants and researchers identifying a story important to the group as well as an audience for whom the story will be important. In its original form, photonovella "featured tableau photographs or still images from films combined with text balloon dialogue" (Emme, in press). Now, as research, it involves the group assembling the story, which is "a collective-creative process of performance tableau and photography, resulting in iconic images, which are then assembled in a comic book–style sequence" (Emme, in press). Photonovella typically appeals to educational and health researchers interested in working with participants situated in institutions (e.g., schools or clinics).

Both the photovoice and photonovella are known as unique research methods for hearing and sharing important stories that communicate "the complexity of research participants' visual culture" (Emme, in press). For example, Emme and colleagues (2006) worked with elementary children, many living in lower income families and many of whom were recent immigrants, to create, reflect on, and respond to photonovellas about their peer relationships. This is primarily a methodological article outlining how the photonovella can be used in research. The authors take the reader through the creation of one photonovella called "Getting into Basketball."

## Community Mapping

Also arising out of PAR is the method of community mapping. Community mapping is a process that invites community members to pool their knowledge and experience of the community and represent this in a graphic form, or map. Mapping involves having community members think through and locate the historical, physical (transportation routes, factory, sanitation stations, shops), social (e.g., community center, community agencies, recreation fields), cultural, and spiritual attributes, including cherished places or landmarks within the community. The process of mapmaking enables community members to establish collective goals about the future of their social and physical environment and how they want to attain these goals. Although typically most time is spent on mapping resources and assets, some might be spent mapping out the values members hold as a community. As in all participatory approaches, it is as much about the process (engaging community members) as it is about the product (the map).

Although it is a relatively new method, the process of community mapping is well established and documented through the work of Canadian Clyde Hertzman and the Human Early Learning Partnership (Hertzman et al., 2002). One project, called the Community Asset Mapping Project (CAMP), maps (e.g., economic characteristics, child care, literacy, and parenting programs) various neighborhoods in Vancouver, Canada, and examines the opportunities and constraints children experience growing up in these various locations.

## Grounded Theory

Barney Glaser and Anselm Strauss initiated a transformation within the social sciences through their book *The Discovery of Grounded Theory* (1967). In it they argued against the dominant view that quantitative study was the only form of systematic social scientific inquiry. With their work rooted in symbolic interactionism, they asserted that scientific inquiry and the building of midrange theories was possible through an inductive approach to collecting and analyzing data (Charmaz, 2000). A midrange theory could be identified through a *basic social process* and a *core category*. They called this approach grounded theory. Essentially, they believed that the only way in which everyday social life and theory can be closely related is if theories are *induced* from the data. As a result, they proposed the analytic technique of constant comparison. Through line-by-line coding and the use of gerunds ("ing"),[5] categorizing, memoing, and theoretical sampling, grounded theory can reveal the processes of human action or experience through their various stages and phases over a period of time (Charmaz, 2006).

As Glaser and Strauss continued their careers, however, they conceptualized grounded theory quite differently from each other and developed different ways of approaching it. Yet as new theoretical perspectives have emerged, both of their approaches to grounded theory have been criticized as positivistic, seeking objectivity and truth. Kathy Charmaz, in *Constructing Grounded Theory* (2006), has balanced the intent of the original method with a constructivist perspective.

Using a feminist grounded theory, Wuest, Merritt-Gray, and Ford-Gilboe (2004) studied how mothers and their children regenerated their families after leaving abusive male partners. This involved replacing destructive patterns of interaction with predictable and supportive ways of being together. This is another example of the authors' theoretical position (feminist) being deliberately named and linked with their chosen method (grounded theory).

In addition to constructivist grounded theory, *situational analysis*, developed by long-time student of Anselm Strauss, Adele Clarke, is an approach to grounded theory "after the postmodern turn" (Clarke, 2005). Situational analysis is a research process that focuses on a *situation* as the unit of analysis and, through three main cartographic approaches (situational maps, social worlds/arena maps, and positional maps), details the elements and relations characteristic of the situation. The emphasis on a basic social process (action) in grounded theory is replaced by a situation-centered framework in situational analysis. Situational analysis involves mapping "key elements, materialities, discourses, structures and conditions that characterize the situation of inquiry" (Clarke, 2005, p. xvii). Situational analysis, because it draws together various areas of study ("discourse and agency, action and structure," "history and the present," etc.; p. xxii), is especially useful for multisite research projects.

In her book, Clarke (2005) provides many examples of approaches to mapping narrative, visual, and historical discourses, accompanied by numerous helpful illustrations. For example, she walks the reader through the development of situational maps (including situational, social world/arena, and positional) of the RU486 narrative discourse. (RU486 is a nonsurgical abortion technology that expels the conceptus from the woman's body similarly to having a miscarriage.)

In a new book, Morse, Stern, and colleagues (2008) come together as key grounded theory methodologists and outline the history, principles, and practices of their approaches to grounded theory. If you are committed to using grounded theory, but require clarification on the various approaches and particular areas of divergence, this book may be helpful.

## Phenomenology

In the late 19th century, phenomenology grew out of Husserl's (1964) concern that "the scientific method, appropriate for the study of physical phenomena, was inappropriate for the study of human thought and action" (cited in Bernard, 2000, p. 20). Since Husserl's time, various schools of phenomenology, each one embracing different philosophers and interpretations of their work, have been established. Phenomenologists seek guidance from existential philosophy to study lifeworld and lived experience for the purpose of "gaining a deeper understanding of the nature or meaning of our everyday experiences" (van Manen, 2001, p. 9). The crux is that it is the study of a prereflective lived experience, or what we do automatically, without thinking about it. It is the experience, not as it is *thought* to be but as it is *lived.* The researcher is unlikely to have a specific research question before entering the study but, instead, begins the study and develops the research question as the inquiry proceeds. Data sources include anything that will provide insight into the human experience, including interviews, diaries, poetry and art, short stories, and other sources. It is also possible to conduct a phenomenological study without interviewing, relying instead solely on literature or art, for example. The end result of a phenomenology is thick description of the meaning, or essence, of the phenomenon, or lived experience.

Austin and colleagues (2005) took a phenomenological approach to study moral distress among psychologists practicing in psychiatric and mental health care sites. Moral distress is described as "one's reaction when one believes one knows the right thing to do but does not do it" (p. 198); in other words, how do psychologists respond when they want to do something that they consider morally right and necessary for a particular client but are constrained by such factors as institutional demands, team conflicts, and interdisciplinary disagreements?

## Narrative

The central tenet that draws researchers to narrative is how stories and storytelling make meaning in our lives. Emerging out of the humanities, narrative is based on the premise that any one person's story, analyzed in sufficient depth, represents a larger collection of social experiences. Through the intense study of the experiences of one or more participants, primarily through unstructured interviews, a story is told. Some scholars have used particular frameworks to analyze their narrative work. For example, Labov and Waletzky (1967) analyzed narratives according to six components (abstract, orientation, complicating action, evaluation, result or resolution, and coda), coding anecdotes, exemplars, and such. Burke (1969) has listed five key elements of a story, and Gee (1991) has looked at strophes, stanzas, and lines (see also Leiblich, Tuval-Mashiach, & Zilber, 1998). However, most narrative scholars do not follow any prescribed framework but instead use theming as their basic analytical technique. The end result of a narrative study is a story of participants' stories. Although I distinguish *narrative* as the method and *story* as the means by which people tell about their lives, not all scholars accept this delineation; Paley and Eva (2005), for example, make a much stronger distinction between these two terms.

In *The Wounded Storyteller*, Arthur Frank (1995) has presented a narrative of ill people's experience and the "bond of suffering that joins bodies in their shared vulnerability" (p. xi). Frank tells of the need of ill people to tell their stories, the embodiment of these stories, or how they are told through a body that is wounded, and how social context influences what and how stories get told. He also distinguishes between the illness experience in modern and in postmodern times.

## Case Study

Case study is an approach to understanding a bounded system. It is not, however, "a methodological choice, but a choice of what is to be studied" (Stake, 2005, p. 443). In other words, if a case study *approach* is chosen, a method through which to understand the case must still be decided, and it can be qualitative, quantitative, or mixed method. The focus, though, is on the *case* and understanding the complexities of it; for instance, a project, program, organization, or particular individual's case. Obviously, approaches to conducting a case study vary, but if the case were, for example, a methamphetamine program, the focus might be on the history of the program, the physical setting, other contexts in which the case is situated (e.g., economic, political, legal, aesthetic), and/or other cases through which the case is recognized (Stake, 2005).

In a qualitative case study of two prestigious midwifery services in the United States, Goodman (2007) has documented the marginalization of certified nurse-midwives. The findings, embedded within a political-economic argument, demonstrate how these institutions modified maternity care and shrank midwifery services without justification.

## Discourse Analysis

Interest in discourse analysis is rapidly increasing, as we now appreciate language as a form of power. Although discourse analysis has been taken up in numerous ways, its central tenet challenges the assumption "that language is neutral and transparent" (Wetherell, 2001, p. 392). Furthermore, Foucault (1978/1990), in the context of the history of sexuality, has asked us "to account for the fact that it is spoken about, to discover who does the speaking, the positions and viewpoints from which they speak about it, the institutions which prompt people to speak about it and which store and distribute the things that are said" (p. 11).

Questions to ask of a text through discourse analysis include: "What were the most immediate, the most local power relations at work? How did they make possible these kinds of discourses, and conversely, how were these discourses used to support power relations?" (p. 97).

Cheek (1997) has examined the way in which newspaper and magazine articles discursively conveyed and constructed toxic shock syndrome between the years 1979 and 1995. She described how discourses of concealment, scientific/medical frame, and individual responsibility have determined how the debate, the disease, and the women it affects are understood.

Another interesting piece of work was completed by Hodges (2007), who analyzed an interview with U.S. vice-president Dick Cheney to understand the "war on terror" discourse. He specifically examined how the connection between Iraq/al Qaeda discursively unfolds at the micro level to contribute to the circulation of truth claims or "commonsense" understanding at the macro level. Although Hodge called this a textual analysis, it can be considered discourse analysis because of how power, embedded in language, is used to create and produce "truth."

## Conversational Analysis

Conversational analysis was born out of ethnomethodology as introduced by Harold Garfinkel in 1967 (*Studies in Ethnomethodology*) and developed in depth from 1964 to 1972 through work done by Harvey Sacks (*Lectures on Conversation*, published in 1992). Conversational analysis is used to understand the processes of communication and talk-in-interaction. You should be careful not to confuse it with discourse analysis. The analytic focus in conversational analysis is on the sequence of related talk, how speakers' roles or identities are formed through their talk, and how particular outcomes of talk are produced (Silverman, 1998). For an introduction to conversational analysis, see ten Have (1998).

Kitzinger (2000) has taken an interesting approach to conversational analysis, arguing for conversational analysis as a useful approach for a feminist analysis, quite to the contrary of critiques of conversational analysis as antifeminist. She has provided the reader with two examples of how conversational analysis can be used to understand refusal in the context of date rape and coming out for gay and lesbians.

## Interpretive Description

In response to the reality that traditional qualitative methods might not always be appropriate for the nursing domain of inquiry, Thorne (2008) has proposed a qualitative method called interpretive description. Thorne appreciated that nurses often need more than description; they need to understand meanings and explanations underlying clinical phenomena that have implications for practice. The result of an interpretive description is a coherent and clear conceptual description (Thorne, Kirkham, & O'Flynn-Magee, 2004) articulated through themes and commonalities that both characterize the phenomenon and account for the individual variations within it: "A good piece of research will make sense of something that clinicians ought to understand." (p. 3). Although interpretive description grew out of a need for the development of nursing knowledge, it can also be useful in many of the applied sciences, such as physical therapy, occupational therapy, education, social work, and human ecology.

Thorne et al. (2004) conducted an interpretive description of heath care communication issues for people living with fibromyalgia. Because of the nature of fibromyalgia, a disease with invisible symptoms and unknown etiology, communication intended to support people with the disease is often tricky. In this study the researchers described, from the perspective of people living with the disease, what they believed to be the most helpful communication practices among the health care providers.

## Descriptive Qualitative

Similar to Thorne, Kirkham, & O'Flynn-Magee's (2004) assertion that traditional qualitative methods (e.g., grounded theory, phenomenology, and ethnography) are not always appropriate for the nursing domain, others (Caelli, Ray, & Mill, 2003; Sandelowski, 2000) contend that many researchers claim a method that they are not really using (e.g., grounded theory, phenomenology, and ethnography) instead of acknowledging the method they are really using, that of qualitative description. It is perfectly correct and acceptable to approach a problem through a descriptive qualitative method if a basic description and summary of the phenomenon is desired (Sandelowski, 2000). The researcher works and stays very close to the data (not highly abstracted) to produce this summary and description. The theoretical perspective for qualitative description is based on general tenets of naturalistic inquiry and may take on "hues" of others (e.g. feminist, ethnographic, etc.), sampling is purposeful, data collection is likely through interviews, and data analysis is a content analysis (Sandelowski, 2000). After working with students over a period of time from various disciplines, many are relieved to realize that they do not have to fit into or herald a particular method, but can conduct a rigorous, useful, and significant study through a descriptive qualitative method.

According to a descriptive qualitative method, Sandelowski & Corson Jones (1996) studied the experience of "choosing" *in utero* fetal testing with women and many of their partners who had positive or unfavorable fetal diagnoses. There were subtle differences in how choice was perceived (and constructed) following the confirmation of a fetal abnormality as: "nature's choice, disowned choice, choice lost, close choice and choice found" (p. 353). The study has implications for psychological wellbeing of and clinical interventions for these families.

## Concept Analysis

A behavioral concept represents a complex of actions, aims, emotions, and perceptions. By asking various and numerous critical questions of a concept, a researcher using concept analysis determines the current state of knowledge about a concept to increase its pragmatic utility for applied work (Morse et al., 1997, 2000b). Through this analysis a concept is decontextualized so that its meaning does not change in different contexts, although it might be perceived and experienced differently. For example, concepts that might be important to study are loss, suffering, anger, frustration, and disappointment. Concepts enable data to be organized and abstracted; they connect science to the world and, in so doing, link theory and research to practice (Morse et al., 1996).

Weaver and Morse (2006) analyzed the concept of ethical sensitivity across many and varied disciplines (e.g., nursing, theology, law, journalism, and women's studies). They delineated and described the preconditions, attributes, and outcomes of the concept and have provided numerous helpful charts and tables outlining the identification of analytical questions; the coding and sorting of the literature; the anatomy, physiology, and maturity of the concept; criteria for assessing analytical questions; and so on. They also outlined and evaluated the pragmatic utility approach to concept analysis.

## Semiotics

Embedded in cultural studies, semiotics is the science of signs. It provides a set of assumptions that enables the analysis of symbolic systems, including language but also encompassing "etiquette, mathematics, music," billboards, and graffiti (Manning & Cullum-Swan, 1994, p. 466). The linguistic message, the denoted image, and the connoted image anchor the analysis. The main assumption of semiotics is that humans communicate through signs, which represent, or stand for, something else. The interpretation of signs is important as signs represent and sustain social relations.

Two famous semiotic analyses by Roland Barthes, the "father" of Semiotics, concern a Panzani (a company that produces pasta, sauces, etc.) advertisement and the cover of the magazine *Paris Match*. In the latter, Barthes (1957/1972), analyzes the meaning of a young black boy giving the French salute and embeds the analysis in French imperialism and the creation of myth.

## Collective Biography

Collective biography is a relatively new method that has grown out of poststructural theory, the memory work of Haug et al. (1987) and autoethnography. Collective biography is created by a group of researchers who work "together on a particular topic, drawing on their own memories relevant to that topic, and through the share work of telling, listening, and writing, they move beyond the clichés and usual explanations to the point where the written memories come as close as they can to make them to an "embodied sense of what happened" (Davies & Gannon, 2006, p. 3).

Memory is not considered "reliable," "fact," or "how it really happened," yet "at every turn we rely on the powerful and flawed capacities we each have to remember and to make sense of what we remember" (Davies & Gannon, 2006, p. 1). By participants talking, listening, and writing, the point of collective biography is to "bring theory into collision with everyday life and thus to rethink, collectively, both the discursive contexts within which our lives make sense and the uses to which we might put theory" (p. 5).

One of the collective biographies shared in the Davies and Gannon (2006) book arose out of concern about the "regulatory discourses and practices of neo-liberalism in academic workplaces" (Davies et al., 2006, p. 79). In this workshop, the group paid particular attention to the body and the expectation in neoliberal workplaces for that body to be machine-like: to go on and on. In this collective biography, the authors share how "bodies might be lived otherwise, against the grain of neo-liberal imperatives" (p. 82).

## Mixed Method

Some researchers have argued that qualitative and quantitative research belong to different paradigms with incompatible ontologies and epistemologies. As such, they believe that qualitative and quantitative research should not and cannot be combined in a single project. Others see the value in combining qualitative and quantitative research and are trying to do so in such a way that the mixed-method project is done well. A mixed-method project is characterized by a core component, which consists of one complete method, that is combined with "supplementary strategies drawn from a second, different method" (Morse & Niehaus, 2007, p. 542). The core component addresses the research question and, even if conducted alone, is complete and publishable (Morse & Niehaus, 2007). The supplemental component consists of strategies added to fill in missing pieces. The supplemental component is not methodologically complete and therefore is not publishable on its own (Morse & Niehaus, 2007). The core component and the supplementary component can be done either simultaneously, expressed as (+), or sequentially, expressed as (→).

For example, Morse and Niehaus (2007) have detailed a QUAL + quan mixed-method project. This QUAL + quan has a qualitative method as its core, but the researcher simultaneously collects supplementary quantitative data. Morse and Niehaus provide an example of a study of friends and family in an emergency waiting room awaiting news of an injured person. A qualitative study exploring these experiences (QUAL) could be conducted as an interesting and important stand-alone study. However, a researcher might like to measure (using a standardized scale) the families' anxiety during this time (quan). Because the sample is small, this supplementary component cannot stand alone, but if the instrument has external norms, scores from the small qualitative sample can be interpreted within the normative population, and the researcher can draw conclusions about how anxious the participants are and add this to the qualitative description. Although I have focused on combining qualitative and quantitative approaches in this discussion, however, you should recognize that mixed method could consist of combining quantitative with quantitative or qualitative with qualitative.

## Summary

The methods presented here provide a start for the qualitative newcomer. There are number methods available to answer qualitative research questions in varied and unique ways. Be wise and creative when choosing a method and enjoy thinking through how different methods might land you in wildly different places, with different findings, creating diverse knowledge with implications for dissimilar audiences.

## Exercise 3.1: Many Methods and the Armchair Walkthrough

The objective of this exercise is to apply each method according to a chosen area of interest and note the similarities and differences among, as well as the results following from, each method. This is best done with a group of two or three.

Revisit the armchair walkthrough exercise described in Chapter 1 and illustrated in Table 1.1. Identify a broad area of interest, for example, living with a chronic illness or the experience of gay youth. With the numerous methods outlined in this chapter and with the use of Table 1.1., design a research study according to each method. Pay attention to methodological coherence or the fit between your ontological and epistemological viewpoint, your theoretical position/perspective, the method you choose, your research question, and so on. Note which methods tend to have similar data collection or analysis strategies, etc., and how each method provides a different result. Note how identifying the kind of result that a method lends itself to (e.g., practice recommendations, action, in-depth description) influences what you will be able to "say" at the end of your research. Identify the cells you cannot fill in to pinpoint areas for further reading.

## Chapter 4

# Research Question and Sampling

This chapter describes the research question in relation to the researcher's assumptions and the pressure to develop the "right" research question. It outlines qualitative sampling as it differs from quantitative sampling and summarizes factors influencing saturation.

## The Research Question

I now return to the pediatric organ transplant surgeons and specialists introduced in the first chapter and their questions: Why do some parents choose not to proceed with a transplant? What is the nature of teenagers' peer relationships prior to and following transplant? What is life like for mothers after their childs' transplant? What is a "successful" transplant, and according to whom? And the one I found most moving: Given the possible growth and development delays following transplant, do parents ever regret their decision to proceed? One surgeon added, "And do I really want to know the answer?"

These are the kind of research questions to which qualitative inquiry responds. They can be complicated, all-absorbing, grueling, and gripping. The answers compel us to think and act in different ways.

### "Coming up with" a Research Question

What preoccupies you? What strikes you as interesting or abhorrent when reading the newspaper? What bothered you about some comment your neighbor made in passing? What personal experience or experience of a close other do you believe needs attention? There is always a story when you ask students and colleagues why they chose their topic and, subsequently, their research question. Refer to Exercise 4.1: An Environmental Scan to help you narrow your research topic.

A research question assists in defining the study's purpose and context and selecting a method. Reflecting what the researcher really wants to explore, the question takes into account the reason for doing the research and the information that is already known about the area of interest (Maxwell, 1996). The research question should be specific enough to provide some boundaries around the topic while broad enough to invite the unanticipated. A research question does not have to be riveting to the nation or solve world peace. It does need to be intriguing to you and at least a few others; contribute to knowledge/theory, policy, and/or practice; and, you hope, pleasing to funding agencies.

## A Research Question to Some and Not to Others

I caution against judging a colleague's research question. What some find captivating or to be a problem, others do not, and that is okay. I do believe, however, that some research questions have a greater need to be asked than others. In other words, what is our society about right now and what is our role as researchers in this society? I am not trying to classify what is moral, but I always try to think through what matters.

A classroom example illustrates the point. Say the discussion focuses on a woman's experience giving birth. Some students want to understand the social construction of gender in the hospital and to consider the labeling of women throughout medical history as inferior, as "hysterical"; others just want to take the pain away. Both are timely issues, important to women, and acceptable as research topics. Or are they? What is moral and what matters, I am constantly reminded, is truly in the eye of the beholder.

Not liking each other's research questions is just fine, but bear in mind that when we react, it is not so much to the question per se but to the assumptions underlying it.

## Exploring Your Assumptions

Research questions are embedded in our disciplines and personal histories and form the basis for our assumptions. Assumptions are assertions about a topic that we believe to be "true" and according to which we function in our everyday lives. Assumptions may provide a foundation from which to develop a research question or even launch a research program. It is critical to explore your assumptions surrounding a topic and underlying a proposed research question. This might seem trite—at least until you are challenged to think otherwise—but let us think through this scenario.

The topic is access to health care. A student shared that she cannot get a family physician for herself or her children as general practitioners are not accepting new patients. Beyond her personal experience, there are media reports and government documents, including various documents from the American and Canadian medical associations reporting the shortage of physicians. She becomes interested in studying the process of foreign-trained physicians attempting to have their credentials recognized in order to practice. If she can study the process, she might find a way to alleviate some problems within the process and subsequently make recommendations that will enable more foreign-trained family physicians to practice in these countries. The assumption in this scenario is that there is a shortage of general practitioners in the United States and Canada.

This student presents her research question in class, only to find that another student challenges her. Are we really experiencing a shortage of general practitioners, or is the role that nurses play in our health system the issue? Is it about permitting nurses to perform tasks that are currently considered medical tasks and under the control of physicians? For example, could nurses deliver babies, give anesthetics, order or complete tests like blood work and mammograms, and write prescriptions such as those for painkillers or antibiotics? This might ease the physicians' workload and help relieve the shortage.

The first research question was not wrong or unworthy of being posed. The point that I am making is that it is important to study your assumptions as they can lead to very different questions. The first student will proceed with studying the process of foreign-trained physicians attempting to have their credentials recognized. The second student will examine the structure of health care and the power of medical organizations to lobby for their continued role as gatekeepers of the system and to define legitimate medical knowledge. Both students are interested in the topic of access to health care but are asking very different research questions based on their assumptions concerning where the problem lies.

## Choosing the "Right" Question.

Spending time thinking through and determining a research question is difficult and important and needs to be done to a greater or lesser extent, depending on your method (e.g. more for a grounded theory and less for a phenomenology). A research question helps decide the purpose and the boundaries of the study. When you feel sideswiped by an external other who asks, "Why did you not examine this or that?" you can often go back to your research question and confidently, and perhaps a bit smugly, state, "That was outside the purpose/intent of my study." So having a good research question really does help in practical ways.

But I get worried when students spend days, months, and—yes—years trying to find the "right" research question. Choosing the right question seems to consume them until one day they emerge, haggard, with a thesaurus in hand, and announce, "I finally have it!" as if the thesis will now write itself. Choosing a research question should not be this laborious and should not hinge on how clearly defined supervisory committees or funding agencies believe a research question needs to be before you can proceed with the research.

The reason I am not advocating the year-long approach to determining your research question is the exploratory nature of qualitative inquiry. No matter how long you spend preparing, things rarely go as you have laid out in your proposal. The participants you chose (new police officers) did not have the time or interest to speak with you; the timing of when you asked participants about the phenomenon was all wrong (you asked them about high-risk decision-making just after the car chase); the setting was all wrong (you thought that you would conduct interviews at the station, but people kept interrupting); or the data demanded to be treated like a narrative, not a grounded theory as initially conceptualized (you need to write the story of the experience of being a new police officer, not break it down into the stages and phases of the experience).

So your research question might change. Clearly, this is unsettling to many funders, supervisors, and students, yet it is one of the privileges of qualitative inquiry. Not changing your research question when you clearly need to is also called "beating a dead horse," meaning that you have continued doing something long after you should have stopped (i.e., collecting data to try to answer your unanswerable research question). It is also a threat to the rigor of your study.

Here is an example. A student wanted to study the experiences of Chinese elders as they accessed the Canadian health care system. She started data collection during the outbreak period of severe acute respiratory syndrome (SARS). What did the participants speak about? SARS. No matter how hard she tried to get them to talk about accessing the health care system, get them "back on track," as she was so aptly taught, they were preoccupied by SARS. In the end, she listened to her data, changed her research question, and entitled her study *The Responses of the Elderly Chinese in Edmonton to the Threat of SARS* (Wills, 2005).

My doctoral dissertation was on the implementation of a policy in government. I conceptualized the study while one leader was in office, but before I started data collection, a new leader was elected. He began a radical restructuring of government and an overall questioning of what the business of government is. When I interviewed bureaucrats, policy implementation was not on their minds. They spoke about what it was like to be a bureaucrat at this time of radical restructuring. My question changed from something like "How are policies implemented in government?" to "What is it like to be a bureaucrat in government at a time of radical restructuring?"

So labor all you want over the "right" research question, but it is likely that the research question, along with other aspects of your study, will change as you proceed. It is also possible that your research question will be the last thing you write.

## Sampling

Nothing highlights the difference between quantitative and qualitative methods more explicitly than the logic that underlies sampling. The aim of quantitative sampling is generalization to the larger population based on random sampling and statistical probability theory. The aim in qualitative sampling, on the other hand, is to understand the phenomenon of interest in-depth. Quantitative random sampling controls for selection bias, which, if is not controlled, would be a weakness of the study or a threat to rigor. Bias in qualitative research, on the other hand, is a sampling strength.

Qualitative inquiry depends on samples that are selected purposefully, a practice that can be applied not only to people (for interviews), but also when choosing documents, images, and so on. The researcher chooses individuals and contexts by asking: "What kind of characteristics of individuals am I looking for?" "Who can give me the most and the best information about my topic?" "In which contexts will I be able to gather the most and best information about my topic?" The researcher then selects individuals (or other data sources) and contexts from which a great deal can be learned about the phenomenon (Morse, 1991b).

Here is an example that illustrates the difference between random sampling and purposeful sampling. If a researcher wishes to understand conflict within faith communities (see Wall, 2002), a quantitative approach would require him or her to select a sample randomly from all registered church members belonging to a particular denomination so that everyone in that particular population has a chance to participate. The researcher could then send those randomly selected individuals a questionnaire structured around the experience of conflict within a faith community. The use of a questionnaire presupposes that the researcher knows enough about the experience to be able to craft questions for the questionnaire, in this case questions that are aimed at managing conflict.

More likely, however, the researcher would take a qualitative approach and choose purposeful sampling by asking: Who would provide the best information about the topic? In which contexts would the most and best information be found? The researcher would possibly interview people who identified themselves as active members, including leaders, of a faith community about their various experiences with conflict within that community, the ways in which it was managed, and what it meant to them and others in the community. If the researcher wanted to do a comparison study, the same questions could be asked in philosophically/ theologically different faith communities. After identifying the constructs important to this phenomenon, a survey could be developed that other faith communities might use to understand conflict within their communities and therefore move into a quantitative design.

Likely, *purposeful sampling* will be the strategy you use in your study. However, other sampling strategies are also available in qualitative inquiry. *Theoretical sampling* involves "seeking pertinent data to *develop* your emerging *theory*" (Charmaz, 2006, p. 96; emphasis in the original). The purpose is to "elaborate and refine the categories constituting your theory" by developing the properties of each category until no new properties surface (p. 96). This strategy is core to grounded theory. *Convenience sampling* is another very common sampling approach that qualitative researchers use wherein participants, documents, images, and so on, are selected simply because they are the only ones available to the researcher (Richards & Morse, 2007). For example, convenience sampling would likely be the approach if you are studying the experience of children with cancer.

If you would like more detail or information on a specific strategy, Patton (2002) has provided a comprehensive list of sampling strategies, including extreme or deviant case (outliner) sampling, intensity sampling, maximum variation sampling, homogeneous sampling, typical case sampling, critical case sampling, snowball (sometimes called chain or nominated) sampling, criterion sampling, theory-based sampling, operational construct sampling, and theoretical sampling.

## Saturation

When should you stop collecting data? The formal answer is: when you have reached saturation; in other words, when no new data emerge, when all leads have been followed, when negative cases have been checked, and when the story or theory is complete. This is somewhat artificial as new and unique information consistently enters the research, but there comes a time when doing another interview or analyzing another document or image is not helpful.

So a question that graduate students inevitably ask is: "How many people do I need to interview to reach saturation?" Although there is no one exact answer to this question, we can anticipate numbers based on experience with different methods. In other words, how many participants does a phenomenology typically require? The best way for you to answer this is to ask a knowledgeable colleague and/or read similar phenomenological articles (or your chosen method) and find out the number of participants reported. Morse (1994a) also provides a guideline (with her emphasis on guideline) for sample size for some common methods.

But this is just the beginning of understanding sample size and saturation. Morse (2000a) has outlined several factors listed below that relate to saturation for interviews. Although these factors refer to interviews, they can also be applied to other forms of data (e.g., observation, images or documents) and include:

- The quality of data: Saturation is more easily obtained if the quality of data is good—whether the interview was recorded, if the recording (or image) was clear, if you had time to make detailed field notes, if the transcripts were cleaned (accurate as checked against the original audiofile)—and so on.

- The scope of the study: If the scope of the study is limited, saturation will also come earlier. For example, saturation will be experienced sooner if the study is about parents' opinions of the new sexual health curriculum for grade 4 students (narrow scope) than if it addresses parents' opinions of the new sexual health curriculum implemented across the grades (broad scope).

- The nature of the topic: The nature of the topic or the degree to which participants can speak easily about (or images or other data can easily be gathered regarding) the phenomenon, also influences saturation. For example, it might be easier for participants to speak about their experience caring for an elderly dying parent than to discuss caring for a dying child.

- The amount of useful information: Saturation is also influenced by the amount of useful information acquired from each participant, setting, image, or document. This means that saturation will be experienced sooner if participants, for example, have a lot of experience with the phenomena, can describe their experiences well, and can spend a reasonable amount of time with the researcher describing their experiences.

- The number of interviews per participant: A larger number of interviews per participant, particularly if "good" participants are interviewed more than once and if they speak primarily about their own experiences rather than reporting another's experience ("shadowed data"), will enable earlier saturation.

- The qualitative method and study design used: The qualitative method and study design used will also affect sample size and saturation. As stated above, to learn more about typical sample sizes for particular methods, it is best to review and learn from articles that follow the method you are interested in.

For many people, saturation is a thorny issue, sounding all too "clean" for the complexity of people's experiences and the messiness of qualitative inquiry. Regardless of whether you like the word *saturation* or not, there comes a point when you believe that you can say something about the phenomenon, in whatever form you choose (e.g., art, performance, text). You keep going until you are convinced that you can do this. Indeed, participants keep diverging and saying interesting things, or else more images appear that you cannot quite account for, which makes you start thinking about your next study and the study after that. At this point, return to your research question and ask yourself whether you have answered it to the best of your ability; not whether you have it "right" but whether you have something important to say, to contribute, or to problematize. If that is the case, you have reached saturation.

## Summary

Your research question must be interesting to you, valuable to your discipline, and aligned with the assumptions in both. It should provide some boundaries to your inquiry but be broad enough to invite the unexpected. Your research question should also guide your decisions about sampling and saturation. Without a doubt, the research question carries a heavy responsibility. Pay due attention to developing your research question, but also "enjoy the ride" of your research and remind yourself that if you need to change your research question, it is likely that you are doing a good job (following your data; inviting the unforeseen) rather than a poor one.

## Exercise 4.1: An Environmental Scan

The objective of the environmental scan exercise is to begin thinking about the pressing issues or topics in your area of interest. This is an exercise best conducted on an individual basis.

To conduct an environment scan, speak with friends and colleagues about your general area of interest, observe (watch television), read the newspaper, the literature and blogs, and listen to others (the radio). This will give you a sense of what is being discussed, what is important, and what needs to be done, etc., in your area of interest. Combine this information with your personal opinions and ideas on the topic. List what you consider to be the top three or four issues/concerns in your area of interest. This unbridled list will become tame as you continue to "come up with" your research question.

# Chapter 5

---

# Data Collection

Chapter 5 begins by explaining the shift from the use of the term data collection to data generation or data making. Specific strategies of collecting data are described including interviews (and focus groups as a type of interview), participant observation (and field notes), documents, and visual data. Appendix A provides an example of an approach to transcription, Appendix B shares an example of field notes, and Appendix C offers a template for document analysis.

The title of this chapter is inaccurate: It should be Data Making or Data Generation. Yet the methods section of any thesis or article outlines data "collection." Attention to the tenets of constructivism, feminism, or any "post" perspective has made us more honest about the data collection process. Referring to data as being collected implies that "data preexist, ready to be picked like apples from a tree" (Richards & Morse, 2007, p. 107). We know that we do not initiate a study as disinterested bystanders but, rather, come to it with interests and assumptions. In interaction with the data source we create, or make, data. The researcher must make decisions about where to point the camera, which images to focus on and which ones to scan (and later delete), which sounds to strain to hear and which ones to block out, which questions to ask the interview participant and which ones to let go.

Think about writing field notes. The researcher cannot possibly take down everything that is happening in the setting; he or she must make choices about what and what not to write down. Furthermore, even if it were possible to take everything down, the words chosen to describe the setting are already a representation, or an interpretation, of what is actually happening. The same applies to other data sources. An interview, for example, is not a direct representation of the participant's life but a representation filtered through the participant's relationship with the interviewer and sense of the interviewer's interest. As soon as we interface empirically with scents, touch, sounds, images, and people, we make choices about what will and will not be data.

To demonstrate to my students how we make or construct data, I show my classes an unstructured videotaped interview that was conducted in a previous research project (Morse et al., 2003) of a woman in her mid-forties sharing her experience of having Guillain-Barr disease. When the participant pauses after answering a question, I stop the tape and ask the students to think about what they would ask the participant next and then write it down. We continue through the interview until the students have three or four questions recorded. We then go back to the first clip, and I poll the students regarding what they would have asked the participant at that pause. Questions vary. Some students want more detail about her medical history, some want to ask about her relationship with her husband, and others think they would simply ask her to "go on." Through this exercise, we discuss that, even though we were all working from the same overall research question, how very different the interview would have been depending on who (with his or her interests and assumptions) was conducting the interview.

We make data and, in turn, create or produce knowledge about the phenomenon. However, although it is important to understand the concept of data making, I use and recommend using the term *data collection* to make your writing straightforward and accessible, hence the title of this chapter.

## Data Collection Strategies

There are numerous ways of collecting data. I will review the strategies that the newcomer to qualitative inquiry will likely use—interviews, participant observation, documents, and images.

### Interviews

There is a narrow conception of qualitative data collection as one-on-one interviews. Why is qualitative data collection dominated by the interview? Perhaps it is because it has become a taken-for-granted. Interviewing is everywhere. Physicians interview us about our health behaviors, teachers about our child's learning style, employers about our productivity, and the media about the "breaking" story. And who can forget Oprah, Larry King, and Dr. Phil, who can essentially and publicly ask anyone anything?

## Interviewing Processes

There are many books and handbooks devoted to interviewing. In them you can find chapters on interviewing processes, including "dos and don'ts." Although these processes might seem somewhat unnatural, it is important to start your interviewing learning here.

The interviewing literature includes the processes involved in preparing for an interview and designing interview questions. There is also literature focused on the interviewer that covers how best to present yourself (e.g., perhaps introduce yourself as a mother if you are researching about mothers' experiences) if you want to build rapport and trust as well as good interviewer qualities to possess (e.g., being a good listener, being comfortable with the topic, and knowing one's own perspective) (Bernard, 2000; Rubin & Rubin, 1995). This literature on examining the self prompts readers to consider, among many things, what their assumptions are about their topic as well as what makes it easier and what makes it more difficult for them to conduct the interviews. Rubin and Rubin also list interviewer pitfalls to avoid, for example asking multiple questions at once, changing direction before the participant is finished, or asking closed questions.

Many texts also devote sections to the typical stages of an interview and discuss what to think about and do at each particular stage. Rubin and Rubin (1995, 2005) have set out five stages of an interview, presented below, but warn that they "are not meant as a rigid guide" (2005, p. 121) but instead have been offered to help the new qualitative researcher move through and possibly anticipate difficulties throughout the interview.

Introducing yourself and the topic is the first stage. It centers on putting both the interviewer and the participant at ease through informal chat and by reviewing the topic and how you will use the participant's information.

Asking some easy questions and showing empathy begins the more formal part of the interview. It is about expressing to the participant that you are interested in what they are saying and want to learn from them.

Asking the tough questions or addressing more sensitive topics follows asking some easier questions and is the third stage of the process.

Toning down the emotional level is about ending the interview on a positive note; it is sometimes accomplished by returning to earlier, less sensitive topics.

Closing while maintaining contact involves thanking the participant and usually making a comment such as: "You have given me a lot to think about." It is also recommended that you "keep the door open" by asking participants, for example, if they want a copy of the report or whether you can talk to them again in the future.

To reiterate, it is important to start your learning about interviewing with these basic tips and processes. Once you are familiar with this literature, you will go forth fearlessly and conduct a few interviews and will likely find that you are doing alright. However, after some time you may start questioning the interview experience and realize that the textbook tips that you relied on so heavily might be missing something. Some of your interviewing experiences will not be found in this literature.

## Interviewing Realities

Although it was not written specifically about interviewing, one of my all-time favorite articles is Fine's (1993) "Ten Lies of Ethnography." It brought me solace as I began to question the interview process during my postdoctoral studies, when I was interviewing hospital administrators about their experiences providing culturally competent care. How does one smile through an interview and encourage a participant to go on, when what she or he is saying is repugnant? I encouraged participants, pretending that I shared their views. I felt slimy, but the data were spectacular, I told myself.

It is okay to like some of participants and not others. It is alright to be sympathetic to some of their concerns and not to others. Sometimes you will feign kindness.

In his article, Fine demands our attention with an opening quote from Urie Bronfenbrenner (1952): "The only safe way to avoid violating principles of professional ethics is to refrain from doing social research altogether" (cited in Fine, 1993, p. 267). Fine's ten lies are found in the work of kindly, friendly, honest, precise, observant, unobtrusive, candid, chaste, fair, and literary ethnographers. I will not paraphrase the entire article, but through these categorizations Fine describes how an ethnographer, or interviewer, may, for example, "appear to be a kindly soul" (p. 272), but turn out to be a "fink" (p. 125; referring to Goffman, 1989), "a spy, an undercover agent" (cited in Fine, 1993, p. 272). In other words, we get the participants' data and then use them to promote our own agendas.

It is now time to wade into the research that has critiqued the interview process and the data we think we garner through interviews (see Atkinson & Coffey, 2002; Brinkmann, in press; Ellis & Bochner, 1996; Gubrium & Holstein, 2003; Kvale, 1996, 2007; Mishler, 1986). Although the authors listed here do not advocate ridding our research of interviews, they ask us to think about how our theoretical positions and/or perspectives situate them. They encourage us to consider the limitations inherent in interviews and how issues of authority, reflexivity, and representation live within and beyond the interview interaction (see Chapter 10 for a more extensive discussion of these concepts).

## One-on-One Interviews

A helpful way to think about interviewing has been described by Gubrium and Holstein (2003), who critique all that we have learned from Oprah and from modernist textbooks about how to conduct an interview. The interviewer develops a list of questions aimed at answering the research question, pilot-tests them, and then meets (or phones) the respondent (not participant) at a mutually convenient time and place. The equipment is tested, and the interview begins. Both the interviewer and respondent know their roles: The researcher asks questions, and the respondent answers. The respondent is not active in the inquiry and often asks, "Is this what you want?" The skill of the researcher is measured in her ability to keep the participant "on track."

The assumption of this modernist approach to interviewing is that valuable information lies inside "the respondent" and that the interviewer simply goes in and gets it. The interviewer "collects" the data without disturbing—"and, therefore, biasing or contaminating—the respondent's vessel of answers" (Gubrium & Holstein, 2003, p. 31). The interviewer must remain neutral to avoid any action "that would imprint his or her presence onto the respondent's reported experience" (p. 31).

As I learned about interviewing at this modernist point in our qualitative history, I was shocked and devastated to see my first interview transcripts, as most people are when they see theirs. I was so chatty! Why did I say that? Why did I interrupt participants? Why did I not keep my mouth shut? Why does it sound more like my interview than theirs?

There are two issues here. First, as outlined by Gubrium and Holstein (2003), I was engaging participants in an unstructured conversation, whereby our perspectives were brought together and knowledge was constructed. Second, there are different kinds of interviews. My method and my personal style lead me to conduct unstructured interviews (Richards & Morse, 2007). *Unstructured* interviews, in which the participant shares his or her story by means of one "grand tour" question followed by a few other broad questions, are likely the most common in qualitative research. Another very common kind of interview is the *semistructured* one (Richards & Morse, 2007), in which you have a fair enough idea of what is going on in or with the phenomenon to develop questions about the topic but not enough to predict the answers. *Active* interviewing, within postmodernism, focuses not only on what is said substantively but how the "meaning-making process unfolds" (Holstein & Gubrium, 2003, p. 68).

*Epistemic* interviewing (Brinkmann, 2007), although not a frequently used style of interviewing, is worthy of note. Brinkmann, learning from Kvale's (1996) *lifeworld* interviewing, has critiqued the descriptive "tell us more," "go on," "what happened next" conventional interviewing. Although he acknowledges that it is appropriate and effective for some research, he believes these types of *doxastic* (experiences and opinions) interviews "do not take advantage of the knowledge producing potential inherent in human conversations" (Brinkmann, 2007, p. 1116). In epistemic interviewing, participants do not share their opinions and describe their stories and then leave it to the researcher to interpret them. Instead, they are confronted and challenged by the researcher to give reasons and justify why they believe and say what they do. The account is structured and interpreted together, and the participant is not "left to guess what use the researcher will make of his or her lengthy descriptions and narratives after the interview has taken place" (Brinkmann, 2007, p. 1136).

Electronic surveys have been available for quantitative research for some years, but now *electronic* interviewing is an option for data collection in qualitative inquiry. One-on-one interviews or focus groups conducted via, for example, chat, e-mail or either synchronous or asynchronous forums have all become possibilities through various software packages. With the possibilities available through the Internet, work is starting on how the context influences data construction. For example, Graffigna and Bosio (2006) compared face-to-face focus groups with different formats of online focus groups (i.e., chat, forum, and forum plus chat). They found not only differences between face-to-face and Internet-mediated settings but also differences among the Internet-mediated settings in terms of both content and conversational and relational characteristics of group exchanges (see also Bosio, Graffigna, & Lozza, 2008). The future of electronic interviewing is sure to present new and interesting ethical, moral, and methodological conundrums.

Other kinds of interviews include structured (Fontana & Frey, 2005), oral history (Candida Smith, 2003), creative (Fontana & Frey, 2005), informal (Bernard, 2000), ethnographic (Sherman Heyl, 2001; Spradley, 1979), life story (Atkinson, 1997), cognitive (Willis, 2005), among others. You should be aware, however, that kinds of interviews are by no means mutually exclusive. Basically, the kind of interview chosen depends on the researcher's purpose, questions, method, personal style, and experience and requires varying degrees of researcher involvement.

## Focus Groups

Brainstorming, nominal/Delphi, field natural, field formal, and focus groups are types of group interviews (Fontana & Prokos, 2007). The numerous types of group interviews, however, have been usurped by focus groups. As soon as a researcher wants to interview two or more people at one time, he or she calls it a focus group. A group interview however, can be defined as a focus group only if the interaction among participants is the focal point of both data generation and analysis (Kitzinger, 1994). Because people form their attitudes and beliefs relative to others', the interaction among participants is an integral part of the meaning of the data (Marshall & Rossman, 1995). In other words, you must be vigilant in examining how the group operates as a group. Because of this, you can begin to understand how focus group data are very different from one-on-one interview data and the research questions that would benefit from a focus group and those that would not. A few good examples lie in the history of focus groups.

One of the first published references to a group interview appeared in 1926 (Bogardus, 1926; cited in Morgan, 1997). In the 1940s, sociologist Robert K. Merton and his associates developed "focused interviews" to study people's responses to propaganda and radio broadcasts during

World War II (Merton, Riske, & Kendall, 1956; cited in Morgan, 1997). By the 1950s, recognition that people make consumer decisions in a social context prompted researchers to try to recreate that context through the focus group approach (Patton, 2002). Since the late 1950s, greater emphasis has been placed on other data collection strategies. As a result, the focus group interview was not developed further until the 1980s, initially by market researchers and then by qualitative researchers (Morgan, 1997).

Focus groups consist of approximately six to ten participants who have a shared experience and are recruited to respond, in a moderated setting and in interaction with others, to a prepared set of questions in one topic area (Morgan, 1997). Focus groups can stand alone as the only data collection strategy in a study, or they can be combined with other strategies (e.g., interviews and participant observation). They are also relied on heavily to generate appropriate wording and questions for questionnaire development and/or to follow another data collection strategy to clarify the results (Morgan, 1997).

David Morgan and Richard Krueger (1998) have done significant work to develop and advance our understanding and use of focus groups. In their focus group kit they outline a very practical approach to planning focus groups, developing questions, facilitating or moderating the group, evaluating effectiveness, and analyzing and reporting focus group results. Morgan (1998) offers guidelines on session length (i.e., two hours for ninety minutes of data collection) and incentives, suggests over-recruiting by 20% to ensure six to twenty participants, and recommends approximately three to five groups. In a detailed discussion of the role of the moderator, Krueger (1998) provides tips on managing the focus group encounter, including how to handle certain types of participant behavior (i.e., experts and influentials, dominant talkers, disruptive participants, ramblers and wanderers, quiet and shy respondents, and inattentive participants).

As a researcher you will find it helpful to have a moderator, someone who can draw out richness in the discussion while ensuring that everyone is heard so that you can listen carefully and watch closely. Another tip that is critical for the transcription of a focus group is to have one person taking notes throughout the session while a second person records the order in which participants speak (Morgan, 1997)· Having a moderator and a note-taker is especially important if the focus group is not being videotaped. There are many other helpful tips for planning and conducting focus groups within Morgan and Krueger's (1998) focus group kit (see also Bloor et al., 2001; Greenbaum, 1998; Krueger & Casey, 2000; Patton, 2002).

A great deal of the focus group literature is situated comfortably within the "how to" realm. The newcomer to focus groups, just like in one-on-one interviews, needs to start learning here. The researcher, however, must then also understand the deeper critiques about and developments in focus groups, including the impact of context on data (Green & Hart, 1999), their use in feminist research (Madriz, 2000; Wilkinson, 1999), and as sites of ethically grounded work (Kamberelis & Dimitriadis, 2005). Indeed, more than ten years ago David Morgan called for increased research into understanding and advancing focus groups, yet "the amount of research using focus groups still outweighs the research about group interviews" (Fontana & Prokos, 2007, p. 101). For further reading on focus groups see Barbour and Kitzinger (1999).

I sometimes worry about new researchers or students who want to conduct focus groups. There is an assumption that focus groups are quick, cheap, manageable, and, even more disturbing, easy to analyze. Do not be fooled. It takes an enormous amount of time and money to organize focus groups, including recruiting, confirming participation, securing a space, arranging for honoraria, transportation, and child care for participants (if required), buying doughnuts and brewing coffee, and doing this four or five times over. You should double the estimated time involved if you are working with a hard-to-reach group. If you are paying a transcriptionist, you should budget six to seven hours of transcription time for one hour of focus group time, depending on the quality and kind (audio only or video) of the recording and whether you have notes on the speaking order of participants. A talkative group that is moderated well can be a positive experience for participants and provide excellent data. A difficult group, one that is beyond the best moderator's skill, can be a damaging experience for participants and for the study and provide scanty data.

As in most qualitative analyses, and as mentioned previously, the analysis of focus groups is not well described in the literature. Furthermore, although a common rationale for choosing focus groups, as stated above, is so that the researcher can observe nonverbal behavior and the interaction among participants, these data are rarely the focus of the study. Typically, the research report centers on what was said (through a content analysis) and not the nonverbal behavior or interaction that created or accompanied what was said. Many new researchers treat focus groups as a handy way to access several participants simultaneously (Kitzinger, 2004), making them neither focus groups nor individual interviews.

It is not my intention to scare new researchers away from conducting focus groups. When they are done well, the outcomes can be jolting and different from anything you could have obtained through other data collection strategies. What I am saying is: Do not approach them flippantly. Take the time and energy necessary to make them seem effortless and proceed with caution.

## Transcription

After you have completed a one-on-one interview or focus group interview, you will transcribe it or have it transcribed. Although you cannot underestimate the importance of transcribing your own interviews and how you begin to think about your data as you do it, there is a reality that if you are funded, you will likely hire a transcriber. In either case, developing a key outlining what particular symbols represent, referring to appropriate transcription conventions, is important for your data analysis. Your key will be developed based on your method and question. For example, a conversational analysis transcript looks quite different from a phenomenological transcript. In Appendix A I provide an example of a possible approach to transcription.

In the transcription page header you should include the participant code (name removed and replaced with a number), the number of interviews you have done with this participant, the location and date of the interview, and the page number. These must appear *on every page.* If there are numerous interviewers in a project, you will need an interviewer number as well (e.g., Maria becomes Interviewer 2). For example, Appendix A can be read as follows:

Participant code: 03

Second interview with this participant: 02

Location: Drop-in center

Date of interview: January 28, 2008

Interviewer: 2

Page number: 1

In addition to providing information in the header, each line should be numbered so that if you are provided with the header information and line number, you can find exact quotes. To make the transcript easy to read and ensure enough space for notes and/or memos, it should be double spaced with a wide left or right margin.

You also have to decide about making your transcripts anonymous by removing names, titles, job positions, places, and other identifying information. I recommend, if possible, leaving names, places, and so on in the transcript as they provide necessary context. However, if you promised anonymity, you must remember to remove these identifiers in any sort of publication.

Beyond transcription conventions, it is important to be familiar with the critical perspective as it has been applied to interviews and how it can be applied to the processes of transcription, including examining the epistemological assumptions underlying the transcription process and how the transcriptionist influences the research data. For more detailed work in this area, please see Lapadat (2000), Lapadat and Lindsay (1999), Poland (1995), and Tilley (2003).

## Participant Observation and Field Notes

Participant observation is the process of personally participating in the research setting. It was developed initially as a data collection strategy among anthropologists studying foreign cultures early in the 20th century, and, although it is primarily a data collection strategy within ethnography, it is also used in many other methods.

Participant observation can help the researcher access everyday life that is otherwise unavailable through other data sources, including interviews. For example, if you are interested in fanatic behavior at sporting events, your ability to capture the experience is enhanced if you can see how the behavior unfolds as it occurs rather than interviewing someone about his or her sporting event behavior retrospectively. Participant observation can occur almost anywhere, including, for example, hospital units, schools, religious communities, athletic clubs, conferences, shopping malls and grocery stores, and professional corporations. As you participate and observe, the goal is to gain understanding of why people do what they do within that particular setting.

### Writing Field Notes

If you use participant observation, you will describe, as well as you can, that which you observe in the setting. These recorded observations are called field notes. Field notes should describe the researcher's reflections, feelings, ideas, moments of confusion, hunches, interpretations, and so on, about what is observed. Some researchers—and I include myself here—argue that field notes are used exclusively in participant observation. However, others use the term more broadly in reference to all notes recorded in a research setting, for example notes recorded after an interview.

In many qualitative courses professors have their students choose a public place, spend ten or fifteen minutes taking notes on what is going on in that space, and then write a summary that includes some of the interesting things observed. I have provided more details about this exercise at the end of this chapter (see Exercise 5.1: Observation and Field Notes). At a football game, for example, some students will record the physical layout of the stadium and describe the lighting, the seating, and the signs, whereas others will attempt to record the conversations among the fans in his or her section as quickly and accurately as humanly possible. The questions I pose to follow-up are provided in Exercise 5.1. Typically, students are surprised with the markedly different ways they approached this exercise, yet they agree on one thing: It is very, very difficult.

How *do* you record "what is important" in the setting? Just as there are how-to guides for one-on-one interviews and focus group interviews, there are guides for conducting participant observation.

Schensul, Schensul, and LeCompte (1999) have suggested that "to make sense of the bewildering array of new visual, aural, olfactory and social stimuli in the field, ethnographers usually start by observing settings," observing and tracing events, counting and mapping, and "searching for indicators of socioeconomic difference" (pp. 96–97). LeCompte and Preissle (2003) provide a helpful framework for directing participant observation. Selected questions (pp. 199–200) included in the framework are:

1. *Who* is in the group or scene?

2. *What* is happening here? What are the people in the group or scene doing and saying to one another?

3. *Where* is the group or scene located?

4. *When* does the group meet and interact?

5. *How* are the identified elements connected or interrelated, either from the participants' point of view or from the researcher's perspective?

6. *Why* does the group operate as it does?

Although you can follow a template, as mentioned previously, field notes are not data that *really* happened, and quotes are not exact. Even if we are present in the setting, there are some things that pass us by because we are not trained to see them, we are not knowledgeable enough about the setting to see them, or we were simply too tired to note their occurrence (Fine, 1993). In all likelihood, you may start with a template, but as you spend more time in the field, you will develop your own approach and style. As well, you always have your research question or main interest to put boundaries on the process of taking field notes. Please see Appendix B for an example of field notes from a colleague, Lynn Eldershaw,[6] taken during an initial visit to a faith community.

Morse and Field (1995) offer sage advice that is critical for writing field notes. They recommend recording one's notes as soon as possible after the observation, avoiding the discussion of observations until they are recorded, finding a private place that has the equipment required to do the work, planning enough time for recording (e.g., one hour of observation can take three to six hours to record), and avoiding editing while writing. In other words, just write.

In addition to field notes, a researcher might keep a log or field diary for recording daily schedules, interviews, locations of various observations, and expenses. This might be useful later when reflecting on the whole study. A personal journal, or "notes on notes," can also be maintained for recording the researcher's personal reflections, mistakes, and successes. It will be an account similar to the one presented in "Ten Lies of Ethnography" (Fine, 1993). They are data, but not data the researcher wants her or his committee or others to peruse. Students especially should keep a personal journal to which not even a supportive committee member is privy.

## Types of Participant Observation

Four types of participant observation are frequently identified in the literature: complete observer, observer as participant, participant as observer, and complete participant. Again, although this schema rarely reflects what actually happens in the setting, it is helpful to start thinking about the degree of involvement a researcher can have in a setting.

You might, for example, be interested in work and gender and the role of administrative assistants in large corporations. A *complete observer* will observe the situation without engaging in the day-to-day activity.

The researcher would sit in the assistant's office and watch the activity but not interact. Although we can imagine that this could happen, the longer you are in the setting, acting as a complete observer becomes quite artificial. You are watching people, not mice. The *observer as participant* will primarily watch the situation but will also be involved in the activity on a secondary basis. In this case, the researcher could answer the phone if the administrative assistant were busy and put the person on hold until the assistant could answer the call. The *participant as observer* will be fully involved in the daily activities but take time to record observations. The researcher could assist the assistant with photocopying, answering the phone, and responding to management's requests, and so on. The *complete participant* will be fully immersed in the setting so that eventually people start seeing the researcher as part of the organization and forget that he or she is participating as just that: a researcher.

The type of observation used by the researcher and the nature of the setting will determine the format of the field notes. Sometimes it might be appropriate to take extensive field notes while something is occurring, yet this may be completely inappropriate at other times. During these times, the researcher might discreetly jot down brief phrases or even single words at a time. These "jottings" (Morse & Field, 1995, p. 112) will serve as reminders of the observation when the researcher makes an expanded and permanent record of the day's events. Ultimately, the type of participation can vary during the study, and the length of time spent in the setting will depend on the purpose of the observation and the questions to be asked.

The four types of participant observation example above are pretty "clean." We generally choose research questions, however, that come from personal experience and that lead us to research settings and phenomena of which we are a part. Nurses want to study nursing units, teachers want to study the classroom, soccer coaches want to study the team, and people recovering from anorexia nervosa want to study anorexia. But can a teacher study her classroom? Can a coach study team building?

These questions bring to bear the insider-outsider debate. For years, researchers had to state whether they were "insiders" or "outsiders" and list the benefits and disadvantages that would be had as a result. Typically, insiders would state ease of access to the setting and ability to build rapport as well as shared understanding and language. Outsiders, on the other hand, would admit that they might struggle with access and rapport but, to their advantage, could question taken-for-granted assumptions and openly query meaning behind behavior. Rubin and Rubin (1995) have given an example using language. An insider to a setting might hear a participant use the word *pig*, know that the participant is referring to a police officer, and not get sidelined by the word. An outsider to the setting, in contrast, might hear "pig" and, on realizing that the participant is not referring to a barnyard animal, figure out what pig means (e.g., a forbidden food, a person who eats too much, a person who drives using too much of the road, or a police officer). Few assumptions are made of why people do and say what they do and say. In the end, the strength of one position is the disadvantage of the other: Familiarity (i.e., insider) and ignorance (i.e., outsider) produce different results.

## Moving on from "Insider" and "Outsider"

The strictly insider or outsider issue is now passé. We realize that no researcher can truly be an insider or an outsider. This insider-outsider role, instead, sits on a continuum and changes and is negotiated as the study progresses. At one moment, a researcher could be an insider and, in the next, an outsider. For example, a young Egyptian American woman,while studying in Egypt moves from being an insider (i.e., someone who looks the same and speaks the language) to being an outsider when she does not attend mosque and observe the Muslim practices associated with Ramadan (see Sherif, 2001). A black female academic who interviews other black women is an insider as a result of their shared ethnicity, gender, and language but simultaneously has outsider status because of her lighter skin color (see Merriam et al., 2001). In other words, we are complex human beings, yet we ascribe insider or outsider status and assume commonality of experience based typically on one characteristic or demographic dimension of ourselves.

Because of these experiences, it can be argued that researchers who consider themselves more as insiders actually have to be more careful in the research setting than outsiders as they might have more to lose. If they are assumed to be the same as the people they are studying (i.e., insiders) but through the course of the study demonstrate to their participants that they, indeed, hold different values (e.g., on marriage) or do not know the language well, for example, the penalty could be rejection. Outsiders, on the other hand, by being different can get away with asking "dumb" questions. However, the risk is keeping the data at a superficial level (noting the obvious) and possibly frustrating participants through their ignorance. You must think about these trade-offs when thinking about your relationship to the setting and participants and be prepared for a possible identity crisis.

Power is another issue to think about with respect to the insider-outsider continuum. The literature often reminds us that researchers have power, and we need to be aware and cautious of how we can assert power over our participants. Yet power is fluid in these situations, too. The young, educated Egyptian woman has some power because of her American studies, loses her power when she is found not to be married, but regains it when she begins to dress in ways considered more appropriate by participants (i.e., makeup, fashionable hairdo, gold jewelry, veil) (Sherif, 2001). Merriam et al. (2001) explain how a black female academic has power in some contexts, but describe how power shifts as her participants tell her how to run a business (a more valued activity to them than study) and what to write in "the book." It is incorrect to assume that researchers always have the power in all situations.

In the end, it is extremely important to think through the assumptions we make about access to the setting, who holds power, and commonality of experience (Merriam et al., 2001), and how this will change and be negotiated throughout the research. Yet one overriding factor in participant observation continues to be important in this discussion, and that is trust. Trust is gained through the researcher's disposition. In the book *Sidewalk*, Mitch Duneier (1999), a male, white, Jewish Princeton academic, studied with poor, primarily black, male street vendors in New York. Inside-outsider debate aside, his participants might have wanted to speak with him simply because of who he is as a person (e.g., a nonjudgmental, compassionate advocate). He might simply be a very nice guy who was committed to the project.

Access will likely be enhanced if the researcher can provide a credible and plausible justification for his or her research or if the researcher has some connections to the people in the setting and is ultimately perceived by those in the setting as a decent human being (Lofland & Lofland, 1984).

## Documents

Gathering documents is perhaps one of the most commonly stated data collection strategies, but it is the least widely debated or well understood. Documents can include anything the researcher is interested in, such as policy and procedure guidelines, minutes of meetings, program evaluations, annual reports, products from the media, textbooks, clinical guidelines, and historical pieces. Documents can be important for telling a cultural story, providing the context to the research question, or tracking the development of a project.

It is common to propose selecting relevant documents purposefully and analyzing them, typically through a content or, more recently, discourse analysis. Documents are rarely a stand-alone data collection source. However, documents are an interesting record of a particular perspective of a phenomenon and could be used as single data source for many qualitative studies. They are often easily accessible and available and can be inexpensive and unobtrusive ways of collecting data. They are useful for determining such things as value, interest, positions, political climate, attitudes, and trends. Like most qualitative work, however, gathering and analyzing documents can be very time consuming.

Although there are some open access software programs for document analysis, explicating the process of document analysis is generally overlooked in qualitative inquiry. In Appendix C I have provided a document analysis template that we used to understand the developing relationship between researchers and community partners in a large-scale, long-term, community-based research project called Families First Edmonton (Mayan et al., 2008). The template was developed inductively as the documents were reviewed. Each researcher's template for analysis will be different, depending on the researcher's theoretical position, method, and research question. I have included it to demonstrate the depth of data and other possibilities available through a document analysis.

## Visual Data

The collection of visual data has traditionally taken place within anthropology and through the method ethnography. As a result of rapidly changing technology and the prominence of the visual in our everyday lives, researchers from across disciplines are now using, not only photography, but also video and hypermedia for understanding phenomena. This work is called many things, including but not limited to visual sociology, visual anthropology, visual culture (Pink, 2007), image-based research, cultural studies, photo elicitation, photovoice, photonovella, or digital storytelling.

Visual methods were once argued to be an "objective" approach to capturing reality; however, we now know that the old adage "Pictures don't lie" is outdated and that the visual is no more objective, or subjective, than written text (Pink, 2007). As with all other data collection strategies, the how-to manuals for visual data collection, developed from a modernist or realist perspective, although serving an important role, are now considered prescriptions that "distance, objectify and generalize" (Edwards, 1997, cited in Pink, 2007, p. 5) and detract from the ambiguity and expressivity potentially inherent in the visual (Pink, 2007). Ball and Smith (2007), Banks (2001), Chaplin (1994), and Pink have all addressed issues beyond the how-to.

There are, broadly speaking, three ways to think about visual research (Banks, n.d.; cited in Pink, 2007). First, a researcher can make visual representations or produce images to study society. For example, she or he could study affluence by taking photographs of images of wealth in an upper-class neighborhood (e.g., what is thrown out or considered garbage). Second, a researcher can study preexisting visual representations for information about society; for example, she or he could examine birth control advertisements to explore what they tell us about women and sex in our society. Third, a researcher can collaborate with participants in the production of visual representations; for example, she or he could ask "What is the experience of 'home' in extended care centers?" and could work with extended care residents to photograph the center and make recommendations for a more homelike environment. Because the visual can be so evocative and meaningful, it can entice and inspire people to draw on experiences and think about issues in ways that would otherwise be unavailable to them.

## Summary

There are many ways of collecting data from a variety of sources. Although interviews are a staple of qualitative inquiry, too often we confine our data collection to interviews and, correspondingly, our data source to participants. Be creative and think about data as everything empirically available to us, whether it is the latest best seller, poetry, newspapers, art, film, photographs, video, graffiti, pop culture artifacts, movement, and even sound. If it helps elucidate the phenomenon, "collect" it, consider it, think about it, and proceed with analyzing how and why the data make us think about the world in a new way.

## Exercise 5.1: Observation and Field Notes

The objective of this exercise is to demonstrate the complexity behind the data collection strategy of participant observation and field notes. The first part of this exercise is completed individually; it is followed by a group discussion.

Choose a public place and spend ten to fifteen minutes taking notes on what is going on in that space. Write a one- or two-page summary that includes some of the interesting things you observed. After you have completed this task, come together in a small group and discuss the following questions:

- What types of things did you record in your notes?
- What did you observe that you did not think was important to write down?
- Did you jot information down as key words or did you have an opportunity to write more?
- Did you record direct quotations?
- Did you expand on your notes after leaving the setting?
- In what types of settings and with what topics and/or questions can you envision using participant observation for collecting data? Why would participant observation be appropriate in these instances?
- What could you learn through this data collection strategy that would not be available through interviewing?

## Chapter 6

# Data Analysis

This chapter begins with an introduction to induction, deduction, and abducti on; it introduces the analytic processes of coding, memoing, and theorizing and concludes with a description and example of a content analysis.

A colleague once facilitated a course entitled Inside Analysis, "an intensive investigation into the techniques of analysis and representation in qualitative inquiry" (L. P. Eldershaw, personal communication, May 31, 2007). To accomplish the course objective, she asked colleagues across campus to come to class and present how they did analysis from their perspective or method. These colleagues presented on participatory action research, ethnography, discourse analysis, phenomenology, visual methods, and narrative. Their comments following their presentations were as enriching as the class itself. They thanked her for getting them to think through and wrap words around what they did when they analyze data as they had never had to explicate it before. This is why students, and most everyone, struggle with data analysis.

Qualitative researchers often do a poor job describing or articulating their data analysis processes. "The category emerged from the data" is no longer sufficient. Why is articulating our data analysis process so difficult? Different theoretical positions/perspectives and methods create different data that demand to be treated and analyzed differently. Data come from diverse sources and in different forms. Time is spent in the field. There is text, facial expressions, and art. Creating themes is a very different process from building categories. Analysis processes within each method are unique to the method yet are fluid and flexible. Needless to say, describing qualitative data analysis is anything but simple, but there is hope on the horizon. As this issue gains more attention, increasingly sophisticated qualitative and method-specific texts that detail data analysis are being published.

Ironically, given what I just wrote about the uniqueness, fluidity, and flexibility of qualitative data analysis, what I want to accomplish in this chapter is to provide an overview and some clarification regarding qualitative data analysis. I will do this through a description of induction and abduction and clarification of terms and processes of data analysis that weave in and out of all qualitative work.

# Inquiry as Deductive, Inductive, and Abductive

Quantitative inquiry is primarily a deductive activity. A simple puzzle analogy can benefit this discussion. In quantitative inquiry the researcher has most of the 500-piece Dalmatian dog puzzle figured out and is testing the fit of one or two pieces. In other words, a deductive process involves testing a hypothesis (a puzzle piece) within a preexisting framework or theory (the entire puzzle) to see if it does or does not hold within that framework.

Qualitative inquiry is primarily an inductive activity. The 500-piece Dalmatian dog puzzle has been dumped out on the table, and the researcher must try to make sense of it. She or he will be guided by the border pieces (i.e., the literature and experience), but otherwise the picture is there (i.e., the description of the phenomena), waiting to be rendered. The pieces are tested against each other, over and over again, until the picture (i.e., model, description, or theory) is complete or makes sense. The pieces cannot be made to fit together, pounded down with a strong fist. The pieces that you do not think go together need to be tried and, surprisingly, sometimes snap together perfectly. This process is inductive because it starts with individual pieces or ideas and, as the researcher moves around one piece at a time, making small, incremental analytical steps, an overall composite or theory, or story, or description is created.

Although the puzzle analogy could be critiqued by post sensibilities as the creation of only one right picture/truth coming from data, I find the puzzle analogy helpful for understanding the concept of induction.

Morse (1994b) has described the cognitive process of inductive thinking, moving from comprehending, to synthesizing, to theorizing, and to recontextualizing. Comprehending begins when you start thinking about your topic and your setting and learning as much as you can through the literature. Comprehending continues through data collection and initial stages of analysis and is attained when saturation is reached and you are able to write a detailed and dense description of the phenomenon. Synthesizing is the process of "weeding," merging stories and experiences to describe patterns of behavior, and how people act, react, or connect. It is being able to describe the typical and atypical and providing stories as examples of this generalization. Theorizing is not creating facts; it is making your "best guess." You do it through selecting, revising, and discarding over and over again to find alternate explanations or ways to understand the phenomenon. Theorizing results in the best way to explain your data. Finally, recontextualizing is placing your results in the context of the literature, to note how findings support extant knowledge and to claim new contributions.

Induction is the root of qualitative inquiry. These stages of induction are not meant to be used as a checklist as you move through your research. Instead, think of the stages as part of your job description as a qualitative researcher. The stages help you move from an interest or topic, to working with your data, regardless of its source or form, to making contributions or generalizations for understanding the human condition.

Although we emphasize induction in qualitative inquiry, it is also important to be familiar with the concept and process of abduction. Abduction (not of the alien kind) is not referred to a great deal in qualitative writing, yet it helps explain how qualitative work is actually a cognitive process that blends inductive and deductive reasoning. Abduction "begins by examining data and after scrutiny of these data, entertains all possible explanations for the observed data, and then forms hypotheses to confirm or disconfirm until the researcher arrives at the most plausible interpretation of the observed data" (Charmaz, 2006, p. 186).

In other words, instead of starting with a hypothesis and then testing it by collecting the data (deductive), the researcher collects data and then generates hypotheses as he or she tries to explain the data (abductive). It is a process of thinking about all of the possibilities of the data: making guesses, speculations, and conjectures (i.e., hypotheses) about why the data are the way they are and then checking these guesses out with further (including previously collected) data. If the hypotheses are not well supported, then the researcher considers other possibilities. If the hypotheses are supported and quite plausible, he or she moves on until he or she is satisfied that an overall interpretation of the data is complete.

# Terms and Processes of Data Analysis

The inductive and abductive analytic processes are apparent through a "systematic pattern of data collection-analysis-collection-analysis, ad infinitum" (Morse, 1999a, p. 573) that characterizes most qualitative work. The qualitative researcher collects data, analyzes them, collects more data to fill in gaps, analyzes them, collects more data, and so on. Morse describes working with data as

> the process of observing patterns in the data, asking questions of those patterns, constructing conjectures, deliberately collecting data from specifically selected individuals on targeted topics, confirming or refuting those conjectures, then continuing analysis, asking additional questions, seeking more data, furthering the analysis by sorting, questioning, thinking, constructing and testing conjectures, and so forth. (p. 573)

Through this process, the researcher's understanding grows so that she or he can begin to create models or diagrams of the relationships in the data, make links with the literature, seek relationships among concepts or categories, "or do whatever the method being used demands" (Morse, 1999a, p. 573). There is nothing haphazard, airy-fairy, or unscientific about this.

Although I am attempting to provide a general description of data analysis, I want to also provide clarification of three terms often quietly questioned by newcomers to qualitative inquiry: coding, memoing, and theorizing.

*Coding* has become a contentious issue in qualitative research, and new researchers are confused about what to say about it. Do you do it or not? Some researchers say that they do not "code" and trip all over themselves trying to avoid the term. They do not like the word; I suppose that they think it sounds too prescriptive, positivistic. But we all code. As soon as you interface with your data, work with your data—any data at all—you are coding. When you assign a word to a part of your data, when you write something in the margin of a transcript, when you underline a word in a document, when you focus on a specific part of a visual, you are coding. You can even code, as I do, your responses as data. A code could be assigned to a line, portion, or page of a transcript or document, or to a minute detail or larger portion of an image, or even to the image itself. Coding is the first step in being able to say something about the data, the phenomenon. It is the first step in enabling you to make comparisons among pieces of data. You might not call it, for example, axial, selective, or theoretical coding, but you are working with your data and determining what is important to you and what you have to let go. In other words, if you want to do anything with your data other than leave them in their raw form, you have to code.

*Memoing* is another term that causes new researchers some angst regarding analysis. Because it was first introduced in grounded theory (Glaser & Strauss, 1967), some researchers believe that this term is owned by grounded theorists. It is not. We all engage in memoing, or writing preliminary analytical notes about the data, regardless of what theoretical position/perspective or method we are aligned with. Indeed, we cannot stop ourselves from memoing. As soon as we say, "I wonder if ..." or "Could this be about ...?" or "Does this mean ...?" we are memoing. We are making connections or asking questions about why something is the way it is. We are entertaining theoretical notions about the phenomenon.

Again, memoing looks slightly different depending on your theory/ method. Memoing in a grounded theory might be focused on comparing two categories, whereas in an autoethnography it might include asking questions about how one's experience counters a dominant narrative of the phenomenon. The process of memoing, therefore, does not belong to grounded theory but is, rather, a strategy that is useful across all qualitative theories and methods.

Qualitative researchers also engage in *theorizing*. Essentially, that is our job as researchers, but new researchers often interpret this to mean that you have to build theory. You can, but you do not have to. Theorizing means thinking more abstractly about your data. Even in a descriptive study, you theorize about the concept or event you are describing. Theorizing is moving from the particular instances that make up your data to speculation and possible explanations. It is evidenced through summary or synthesized statements about the phenomenon. You need to theorize to do research, but you can also theorize without building a theory.

## Armchair Walkthrough Example

As we return to our armchair walkthrough from Chapter 1 and note the importance of thinking through a study horizontally, it is visually apparent that each theory and/or method has its own cell, or analytic technique. Let us work through another example. As we can see from Table 1.1 in Chapter 1, the typical analytic technique for grounded theory is constant comparison, and for phenomenology, it is theming.

TABLE 6.1: ARMCHAIR WALKTHROUGH EXTENDED

| Ontology, Epistemology<br><br>Theoretical Position | Method | Research Question | Participants |
|---|---|---|---|
| Interpretivist/ Constructivist<br><br>Symbolic Interactionism | Grounded theory | How do families come to practice and sustain nonconsumption of material goods? | Parents with at least one child under the age of six self-identified as a nonconsumer |
| Interpretivist<br><br>Existentialism Merleau-Ponty | Phenomenology | What is the lived experience of being a parent who practices nonconsumption of material goods? | Parents with at least one child under the age of six self-identified as a nonconsumer |
| Interpretivist/ Constructivist<br><br>Theories of Culture | Ethnography | What is parents' experience of nonconsumption of material goods? | Parents with at least one child under the age of six self-identified as a non-consumer<br><br>Staff from associated organizations<br><br>Others to be identified as the study evolves |
| Poststructuralist | | | |
| Feminist | | | |
| Foucault | Discourse analysis | | |
| Narrative | | | |

Following the interest in reduced consumption, you are interested in the culture of non-consumption that is created within the larger, dominating culture of consumption (see Table 6.1). You want to ask the *research question*: What is parents' experience of non-consumption of material goods? This will be an ethnography (*method*), so you work within the third line of the chart. You align yourself with an interpretivist perspective (*ontology* and *epistemology*) and anchor the study in theories of culture and concepts of ritual, norms, and so on (*theoretical position/*

| Sample Size | Data Collection | Setting | Data Analysis | Results |
|---|---|---|---|---|
| 18 | Interviews | Place of participant's choice | Constant comparison | Model or substantive theory |
| 8 | Interviews | Place of participant's choice | Theming guided by four existentials | Rich description of the essence of the phenomenon |
| 25–35 | Interviews<br><br>Participant Observation<br><br>Documents | Associated Organizations<br><br>Participants' homes | Content analysis | Thick description of the phenomenon |
|  |  |  |  |  |
|  |  |  |  |  |
|  |  |  |  |  |
|  |  |  |  |  |

*perspective*). Your *participants* will be parents who self-identify as non-consumers of material goods with at least one child under the age of six. In addition, you will include and learn from environmental nongovernmental organization, alternative food store, and Earth Day staff. Others may enter your sample if they can teach you about the nonconsumption culture of young families. You know that the sample *size* of an ethnography, because it is made up of many conversational interactions (formal and informal *interviews*), is approximately twenty-five to thirty-five participants. You want to spend time in the field (*participant observation*), but stumble when thinking about how to "observe" nonconsumption. You have a few choices to make. You could spend time "hanging out" at the environmental nongovernmental organizations, alternative food stores, and Earth Day festivals (*setting*) and see what kind of data is there. Or, you may want to "hang out" on a Saturday with the families in your study and see how they structure their activities to be non-consumptive (*setting*). The participant observation component will likely evolve as you learn more about your topic. You will definitely want to review *documents* including the lay literature and pamphlets in related organizations and on Websites. You will be using content analysis for *data analysis*, and your *results* will be a thick description of the cultural norms and patterns of behavior that are created within a culture of nonconsumption juxtaposed within the larger, dominant culture of consumption.

## Two Serious Analysis Errors

There are two serious but very common analysis errors made by new qualitative researchers. The first is collecting and then (subsequently) analyzing data. Many new researchers triumphantly announce, "I have collected all my data. Now I just have to analyze them." The only time it is acceptable to have collected all of your data without analyzing them concurrently is for semistructured interviews, in which many participants are recruited, the questions do not change, all participants are asked the same questions, in the same order, and the answers to each question are studied together. Because semistructured interviews are conducted and analyzed in this manner, more than one person can conduct the interviews and analyze the data. Each question might become a category.

If you are using any other method, you must work concurrently, through an iterative process of data collection-analysis-collection-analysis, and so on. If you do not work concurrently, it is likely that you will end up with quite an ordinary study, adding little to the literature, policy, or practice, because you missed a "gem," for example, in the third transcript. That gem, if you had caught and followed up on it, would have changed the nature of the research altogether. In a study of fathers caring for a child with a gross motor developmental disability, a father might have stated in that third interview that the disability affected his desire to be and play with his child. This idea is very new to this literature but might have been missed if the researcher did not analyze that interview shortly after it was conducted and then follow it up in further interviews. The importance of concurrent data collection and data analysis through coding, memoing, and theorizing cannot be understated.

The second error in qualitative analysis is the use of a theory or a conceptual framework to analyze the data. In this sense, I do not refer, as stated in Chapter 2, to critical or post-theories such as queer, Marxist, critical race, or ethnic theories or to symbolic interactionism. The problem lies when a new researcher takes a theory such as attachment theory or family stress and coping theory and looks specifically for the concepts in the qualitative data that make up the theory. The researcher reads line by line, and if a comment resembles, for example, a stressor event or resources from McCubbin and Patterson's (1982) ABCX model of adjustment and adaptation, it is coded as such, and the analysis continues. What is wrong with this approach? It is deductive. The researcher is working from or testing a theory or model in the qualitative data. This squashes any opportunity for new ideas or notions of the phenomenon to be seen, and, again, the researcher reproduces the ordinary.

## Content Analysis

Because many new qualitative researchers choose methods or approaches that require a content analysis or variation, I will outline this analytic technique here. If these processes seem to make sense to how you might proceed with data analysis, please use this as a template to work from but modify it according to your theory/method and data.

In general, in a descriptive qualitative study or an exploratory qualitative study—what some people refer to as a generic qualitative study—or in an ethnography or focused ethnography the most fitting analytic technique is content analysis. Content analyses can be divided into two different types: manifest and latent. In manifest content analysis, or "bean counting" content analysis, the researcher looks for specific words used or ideas expressed. These are tallied, as offered through numerous software packages and then used to generate statistics on the content of the data. For example, a researcher interested in studying the work life of bureaucrats in local government could count the number of times that a bureaucrat refers to being stressed or uses the word stress. That number could be used to argue the significance of stress in the lives of bureaucrats. This tallying is very reliable: It is easy to go through a text and count the number of times a word appears. However, it is meaningless to a qualitative researcher as the context of the words is not taken into consideration.

Latent content analysis is the process of identifying, coding, and categorizing the primary patterns in the data. The researcher examines the meanings of specific passages or paragraphs within the data and determines appropriate categories. For example, rather than simply noting an occurrence of work stress, she or he would code for the type of stress or the context of the stress. Is the stress related to the number of hours worked, relationships with coworkers, balancing work and family, or something else? Or is the reference to stress indicative of something else going on in the organization? When the term content analysis is used, latent content analysis is usually what is being referred to, and that is my usage throughout this book. Latent content analysis is important to the qualitative researcher because it allows coding of participants' intent within context.

## Coding and Categorizing

The first step is to code the data. Coding, within a content analysis, can be defined as the process of identifying persistent images, words, phrases, concepts, or sounds within the data "so that the underlying patterns can be identified and analyzed" (Morse & Field, 1995, p. 241). Coding is not the process of assigning labels or categorizing the data. This occurs later in the process. Coding is simply the first step by which the researcher becomes familiar with and starts to organize the data.

To begin coding text, the researcher reads all the data, rereads and highlights sections of the text, and makes comments in the margins regarding anything that is striking. These comments might include overall impressions, points of interest, plans for working with the data, and so on. For example, to extend the example of stress in the local government, the researcher might note the various ways in which the bureaucrats describe their tiredness. After coding is complete, the data are ready to be categorized.

Going through the data again, the researcher cuts out the highlighted sections of the text and groups them into categories. In precomputer times, this was literally done with scissors and file folders. Now this can be done using Word or with a designated software program (e.g., N7 or Atlas.ti). To account for the data in a meaningful yet manageable way, the researcher should restrict the number of categories to ten or twelve. Consider this portion of a transcript for studying of the experience of being a bureaucrat in local government:

> I've given up on our current council. They just play it safe and follow the rules. They don't allow any of us to try anything new. We wanted to implement a pilot of this new recreation program and did all of our homework and presented it to them and they just said basically, "Thanks, but no thanks, just keep doing what you are doing." I don't feel like I have any power to do anything interesting in my job. It's totally debilitating.

I coded this excerpt of the transcript with the words "council follows the rules" and "no power." These codes, when collated with similar codes, might have eventually developed into two categories: *Lack of Innovation within Council* and *Lack of Autonomy among Bureaucrats* respectively. An excerpt can be double-coded and thus end up in more than one category. This excerpt would likely be found within both of the categories developed.

Once the data are categorized, the researcher takes each file and reads through the excerpts, ensuring that they all "fit" within the category. The researcher has to be willing to move excerpts around, relabel or dissolve categories, or develop subcategories. Subcategories are created if there are two distinct ideas or perspectives within one category. For example, the category *Lack of Innovation within Council* might consist of two subcategories: *Toe the line* and *Conservative politicians*. Often associated with a content analysis is a diagram illustrating the relationship between categories and subcategories. Figure 6.1 outlines the working stage of a diagram for the example given above. Sometimes data are contrary to what most participants are describing. In a content analysis, and in qualitative inquiry in general, this is often called a "negative case." For example, one bureaucrat might not mention a lack of power or autonomy at all, talking instead about her ability to make decisions and have

**Categories**

**Lack of Innovation within Council**
This category consists of bureaucrats'
descriptions of the ways in which council
lacks originality, creativity, and inventiveness
at the levels of both policy and practice. It is
described through two subcategories.

**Lack of
Autonomy
among
Bureaucrats**

**Sub-
Categories**

**Toe the line**

This subcategory cap-
tures how bureaucrats
believe they must sup-
port what senior officials
support and do so even
if it means disregarding
or ignoring one's own
personal values and
beliefs. Working in local
government means that
you cannot disagree,
speak negatively, or
"make trouble."

**Conservative
politicians**

This subcategory is
described as those
politicians who are "right
wing" and who work
from conventional and
established positions,
seeking out traditional
opinions and ideas, and
publishing documents
from a conservative
perspective. Ideas
that did not fit into a
conservative frame were
not welcomed by these
politicians.

Working
Inductively

**Codes**

council follows
the rules

no power

**Excerpts
from
Transcripts**

"I've given up on our current
council. They just play it safe
and follow the rules. They don't
allow any of us to try anything
new. We wanted to implement
a pilot of this new recreation
program and did all of our
homework and presented it to
them and they just said basically,
'thanks, but no thanks, just keep
doing what your are doing.' I
don't feel like I have any power
to do anything interesting in my
job. It's totally debilitating.

"I've given up on our current
council. They just play it safe
and follow the rules. They don't
allow any of us to try anything
new. We wanted to implement
a pilot of this new recreation
program and did all of our
homework and presented it to
them and they just said basically,
'thanks, but no thanks, just keep
doing what your are doing.' I
don't feel like I have any power
to do anything interesting in my
job. It's totally debilitating.

them passed by a forward-thinking council. When such data exist, the researcher must look for similar cases. If similar cases are identified, then a new category or subcategory is created. If no similar cases are found, then that initial case is considered an anomaly but still must be accounted for in the explanation of the data. For example, you might have figured out that this bureaucrat is a few months away from retirement.

Once the researcher is satisfied that the excerpts in each category are part of that category, she or he writes a summary for each category and subcategory. For example, descriptions for the category *Lack of Innovation within Council, Toe the line,* and *Conservative politicians* are provided in Figure 6.1.

The categories are then judged by two criteria: internal and external homogeneity. *Internal homogeneity* refers to the individual categories. Do all of the data reflect the category and fit nicely into it? Does the category make sense? In the example given above the researcher would ask the following question: Do all of the highlighted sections of text in the file *Toe the line* and in the file *Conservative politicians* relate specifically to that category? *External homogeneity* refers to the relationships among the categories. Are they all distinct and separate? The differences among categories should be bold and clear. The subcategories *Toe the line* and *Conservative politicians* should reflect different and distinctive experiences of bureaucrats. The categories *Lack of Innovation within Council* and *Lack of Autonomy among Bureaucrats* should, too, reflect different and distinctive experience of bureaucrats in local government.

## Forming Themes and Making Conclusions

Newcomers often confuse or do not understand the difference between categories and themes. Themes are thoughts or processes that weave throughout and tie the categories together. Theming, then, is the process of determining the thread(s) that integrate and anchor all of the categories. To form themes, the researcher returns to the "big-picture" level and determines how the categories are related. You will typically have only one to three themes. If you have more, you are likely not abstracting enough. Through the categories and then the themes, the researcher can make overall conclusions about the research (see Exercise 6.1).

Beware of categorizing, theming, and drawing conclusions prematurely. Content analysis, like most qualitative data analysis, is a circular process. After reading an intriguing piece of data that does not fit with other data, the researcher might need to conduct further investigation. The continuous addition of new data might result in changes in the categories and the relationships among them. The researcher must remain open to this happening, which is one of the most difficult parts of data analysis in qualitative inquiry.

## Summary

Given the nature of qualitative inquiry, the processes of data analysis are poorly articulated. It is important however, to think very hard about data analysis and approach it as an iterative abductive process. The researcher's main tools for analyzing data, albeit used and thought about differently depending on the researcher's theoretical perspective and method, are coding, memoing, and theorizing. A content analysis is just one approach to working with qualitative data. However, novice researchers commonly report using a particular analytical technique while actually conducting a content analysis. You can tell when you read the article if they have done so: The analytical techniques lying within other methods (e.g., conversational analysis or discourse analysis and phenomenology) look and feel very different from a content analysis. Although content analysis is a valuable and appropriate analytical technique in many circumstances, it cannot be applied through every perspective or method in qualitative inquiry.

# Exercise 6.1: Categorizing and Theming

The objective of this exercise is to demonstrate the difference between categorizing and theming. Work on this exercise alone or in a small group.

Take a newspaper or magazine article. Code it, categorize it, and list your categories. Answer the question: If I had to make one or two statements about "what I found," what would I say? Take your one or two statements and determine if and how they link to each of your categories. If they do, you have likely identified your theme(s). If they do not, rethink your statements so that they cut across all of your categories.

A more involved categorizing and theming exercise can be conducted by downloading a talk show or political leadership debate transcript or working with a transcript from an actual interview.

# Chapter 7

## Rigor

Chapter 7 discusses the contentious issue of rigor. It provides three options for managing rigor and outlines verification and other strategies for ensuring rigor.

I like rigor. I like talking and thinking about rigor in qualitative research. Rigor is demonstrating how and why (through methodology) the findings of a particular inquiry are worth paying attention to.

Unfortunately, some qualitative researchers are uneasy with or even afraid of pairing qualitative inquiry with rigor. In response to questions about rigor, these researchers freeze, turn red, or avert their eyes from the questioner. This often happens with graduate students, who silently plead during their dissertation defenses that the question about the generalizability of their findings not be raised. Other researchers do not avoid the questioner's gaze; on the contrary, they answer the question with a piercing critique of how rigor is deliberately damaging to what we are trying to accomplish through qualitative inquiry. I will try to make sense of these opposing positions.

## The Rigor Game

The researchers who understand rigor as damaging to qualitative inquiry often refer to rigor as a game. The qualitative researcher is warned to ask: Who wants to play this rigor game, and what do they want to get out of it? Generally, researchers often link rigor with power and positivist thought, which, they argue, produce and reproduce a certain type of knowledge.

The institutions that need to play the rigor game are those whose interests are served through the maintenance of the status quo or certain truths. The rigor game players gain at the expense of those whose realities do not penetrate dominant structures or discourses. Only certain knowledge (and likely not that produced through qualitative research) is allowed in the rigor game.

Of course, qualitative researchers should be apprehensive if rigor is conceptualized and used in this way. Do not accept things carte blanche. You must be aware whose game you are playing and if and how you play into it. Be careful.

This diatribe on the rigor game, however, does little to satisfy students, who remind me of the questions they will face during their dissertation defense. They want specifics on how to talk, do, and write about rigor. I am sympathetic, so I find myself revisiting the basics of rigor and laying out three options.

## Talking, Doing, and Writing about Rigor

The first option is to choose a particular set of criteria that best fits the research. The second option is to use the terms *validity, generalizability,* and *reliability.* The third, a less appealing or viable option for students, is to avoid the use of criteria altogether.

### Sets of Qualitative Criteria

The first option, choosing a set of qualitative criteria, begins with appreciating the influential work of Egon Guba and Yvonna Lincoln. In the early 1980s, Guba and Lincoln (1981) directly tackled the issue of rigor in qualitative research. As they stated, and as many have reiterated since then, qualitative research does not adhere to the positivist paradigm's prescriptions of rigor (validity, generalizability, and reliability), and it is detrimental to apply the quantitative rules of rigor to qualitative research. Consequently, Guba and Lincoln argued for a different way of speaking about rigor in qualitative research and different criteria for evaluating it. In 1981, they proposed using trustworthiness (to replace rigor) with the criteria of credibility, fittingness, and auditability. In 1985, Lincoln and Guba maintained trustworthiness but revised their original criteria to credibility, transferability, dependability, and confirmability as outlined below:

*Credibility* replaces the criterion of internal validity. It assesses whether the findings make sense and if they are an accurate representation of the participants and/or data. Strategies such as member checks, prolonged engagement in the setting, and triangulation of data assist in ensuring credibility (see below for a description of these strategies).

*Transferability* replaces external validity. It assesses the applicability of the findings (being transferred) to other settings and is acquired through the strategy of providing detailed thick description of the setting and participants.

*Dependability* is referred to instead of reliability. It refers to the opportunity, post hoc, of reviewing how decisions were made through the research and is attained through the use of an audit trail.

*Confirmability* replaces objectivity and is used during the data collection and analysis phase to ensure that the findings are logical. The technique is, again, the audit trail, or the opportunity to examine data and resulting interpretations. Confirmability has evolved through the practice of reflexivity. (Lincoln & Guba, 1985)

This important work, published more than twenty years ago, was critical to the development of rigor in qualitative inquiry. It provides the foundation for considering other criteria for judging qualitative inquiry, including Lincoln and Guba's continued work in this area (see, e.g., Lincoln & Guba, 2000). Unfortunately, however, the introduction of qualitative criteria also brought a circus of rigor criteria to town. Scholars have thrown various definitive terms and criteria into the qualitative research ring. On this issue, Pamela Brink (1991) has stated it best: "In the literature on reliability and validity, I find the terminology execrable! We have so many terms to cover the same concept. Nobody is talking to anybody. Anybody who does anything at all on reliability makes up a new term to cover what has previously been discussed in another field" (p. 164).

Brink is right. In my attempts to grasp the field, I created Table 7.1 from just a slice of the literature. I chose work from a range of years to demonstrate the initial and persistent creation of new criteria. The Criteria column, sometimes referred to as standards or attributes, lists the criteria that authors have proposed as important for achieving rigor/ trustworthiness.

This proliferation of qualitative criteria has had negative as well as positive outcomes. On the negative side, the abundance of criteria has been anything but sublime to the qualitative newcomer. Should a text be judged on its clinical or practice implications, or on the meaning of

TABLE 7.1: PROLIFERATION OF CRITERIA

| Author(s) | Year | Criteria |
|---|---|---|
| Guba and Lincoln | 1981 | Credibility, fittingness, auditability |
| Polkinghorne | 1983 | Vividness, accuracy, richness, elegance |
| Lincoln and Guba | 1985 | Credibility, transferability, dependability, confirmability |
| Kirk and Miller | 1986 | Quixotic reliability, diachronic reliability, synchronic reliability |
| Eisenhart and Howe | 1992 | Completeness, appropriateness, comprehensiveness, credibility, significance |
| Maxwell | 1992 | Descriptive validity, interpretive validity, theoretical validity, evaluative validity, generalizability |
| Leininger | 1994 | Credibility, confirmability, meaning in context, recurrent patterning, saturation, transferability |
| Lincoln | 1995 | Positionality, community as arbiter, voice, critical subjectivity, reciprocity, sacredness, sharing perquisites of privilege |
| Thorne | 1997 | Epistemological integrity, representative credibility, analytic logic, interpretive authority |
| Popay, Rogers, and Williams | 1998 | Interpretation of subjective meaning, description of social context, evidence of theoretical or purposeful sampling, evidence of adequate description, evidence of data quality, evidence of theoretical and conceptual adequacy, potential for assessing typicality, relevance to policy |
| Madill, Jordan, and Shirley | 2000 | Internal coherence, deviant case analysis, reader evaluation |
| Richardson | 2000 | Substantive contribution, aesthetic merit, reflexivity, impact, expression of a reality |
| Bochner | 2001 | Detail of the commonplace, structurally complex, sense of author, stories about believable journeys, ethical self-consciousness, moves reader at the emotional and rational level |
| Ballinger | 2006 | Coherence, evidence of systematic and careful research conduct, convincing and relevant interpretation, sensitivity to role played by researcher |
| Finlay | 2006 | Clarity, credibility, contribution, communicative resonance, caring |

the text? Should it be judged on its involvement of participants as co-researchers, or on its theoretical elegance? The large numbers of criteria might also give the impression that we qualitative researchers are uncertain about what we do. Indeed, for more than twenty-five years qualitative researchers have debated, through both quick commentary notes and lengthy texts, what makes a good qualitative study. As Seale (1999) has stated, "The urge to generate criteria for judging good-quality studies seems irrepressible" (p. 43).

On the positive side, the evolution of the initial criteria has reflected changes to and challenges toward dominant thought. It has pushed us as qualitative researchers to deeply contemplate and determine what to aim for in our research. This has prompted the reframing of conventional criteria (validity, generalizability, and reliability) and has led to the development of criteria for ethical, moral, literary, political, critical, and creative intentions. For example, Bochner (2001) has asked us to consider whether there is respect for the moral dimensions of the story. Richardson (2000) has asked: "Does the use of creative analytical practices open up the text, invite interpretive responses?" (p. 254). Finlay (2006) has queried whether the account offers "guidance for future action or for changing the social world for the better" (p. 322). As Richardson (2000) has written: "Increasingly ethnographers desire to write ethnography which is both scientific—in the sense of being true to a world known through the empirical senses—and literary—in the sense of expressing what one has learned through evocative writing techniques and form" (p. 253). Indeed, some of these sets of criteria have enabled brave scholars with alternative approaches to research to be considered seriously.

Yet to be honest with ourselves, we must acknowledge that literary techniques do not apply to qualitative research alone. All research reports are formed through "literary technology" (Shapin, 1984; cited in Sandelowski & Barroso, 2002, p. 6), whereby authors rhetorically use literary devices of many kinds, such as "correlation coefficients, p values, metaphors, coding schemas" and emotive quotes to convince readers to accept their research as good (Sandelowski & Barroso, 2002, p. 6).

If you are considering choosing a set of qualitative-specific criteria in addition to the ones referred to in Table 7.1, others to consider are those set out by Ballinger (2006) and Polkinghorne (1983). However, it is important to realize that these criteria are particular to your research. Although a great deal of effort has gone into the formulation of criteria for establishing rigor (trustworthiness), we will never establish consensus on an overall set of criteria to judge the quality of qualitative research. Why? Because criteria must be chosen that best fit with the research, its epistemological underpinnings, and the discipline within which it is situated. Accordingly, "any work of art—including the research report—must be understood or appreciated for what it is before it can be judged as a good or bad example of its kind" (Sandelowski & Barroso, 2002, p. 10).

A colleague of mine likes to think about the various criteria as an assortment of board games. A researcher may choose from a variety of games (qualitative research designs/theoretical positions/perspectives/ methods) but then must apply the rules or strategies (criteria) of each game to lead them through the game (research). If you apply the rules of Monopoly (e.g., autoethnography) to Risk (e.g., grounded theory), you had better not be a gambling person. But if you apply Monopoly rules to Monopoly, the outcome is likely to be favorable.

Exercise 7.1 (Examining Criteria/Standards) asks you, contrary to my advice above, to come up with, as a group, an overall set of criteria. The purpose of this is for you to appreciate the varying approaches to criteria, perhaps give you insight about some contention, and most importantly, help you identify how you will handle rigor in your research.

## Validity, Generalizability, and Reliability

Before you sort through the various qualitative-specific criteria, it is important to reconsider the core of the argument for using alternative criteria. To reiterate, many qualitative researchers still argue (see Finlay, 2006) from Lincoln and Guba's (1985) contention that because qualitative and quantitative research are associated with different paradigms, different criteria for evaluating research within each paradigm are needed. As initially proposed, qualitative-specific criteria mirrored quantitative criteria (credibility-internal validity, transferability-external validity, dependability-reliability, confirmability-objectivity). The point of the creation of these criteria was to move researchers away from applying the quantitative rules of rigor to qualitative research. But does this require a change in terminology? Can we not use the terms that represent good science (validity, generalizability, and reliability) but apply different rules of rigor accordingly?

Thus, the second option is to use the terms *validity, generalizability,* and *reliability* (see Morse et al., 2002). To be clear, it is the terms that may be used, not the definition of the *terms* as provided from a positivist perspective. We need to think differently, expand our understanding, and reconceptualize the terms *validity, generalizability,* and *reliability* through a qualitative lens. A simple argument demonstrates how they can make good sense in qualitative inquiry.

In quantitative inquiry, internal validity is about whether all of the extraneous variables were controlled so that the independent variable truly produced the observed variation in the dependent variable. In qualitative inquiry, we are concerned with whether the story, the description we give of the phenomenon, etc., are found in the data. The essence in both quantitative and qualitative inquiry is that we have confidence that our conclusions, however unfinalized or problematized they are, come from the independent variable or the data (i.e., the text or images). In other words, we are sure that what we are writing came from our data and not from a vision in the sky.

Generalizability in quantitative inquiry, obtained through an adequate and random sample, assumes that the findings from the sample are similar to those in the entire population and thus permits the effect in the sample to be transferred to the larger population (Morse, 1999b). In qualitative inquiry, on the other hand, participants, images, documents, and so on have been selected purposefully to capture a range of experiences with the phenomenon. They have been selected for the contribution they can make to developing the theory or understanding the phenomenon broadly and in depth. Because the resulting theory or representation has included a variety of experiences, it can be used to understand similar scenarios, topics, or problems. It is "the knowledge that is generalized" (Morse, 1999b, p. 6).

By way of an example, Applegate and Morse (1994) conducted a study of privacy in an all-male nursing home. Respect for privacy was maintained when *people* treated each other, friends or strangers, as people. If people were treated as objects, privacy norms were violated. The findings are generalizable to any setting in which privacy violations are a concern (Morse, 1999b). Think about their applicability to settings such as prisons, boarding schools, and medical units.

In quantitative inquiry, reliability is concerned with replication. If the analytic strategy were repeated by the same or a different investigator, then the results should be the same. Replication in qualitative inquiry comes through as repetition or duplication within the data set. For example, it comes with hearing/seeing, over and over again, similar common experiences among participants, even if there are both common and contradictory experiences in the same data set. It can also be understood through saturation.

Some qualitative researchers report interrater reliability when analyzing their data. In other words, they code their data and then ask someone else to do the coding to determine whether they "saw" the same things in the data. This contradicts some of the basic tenets of qualitative inquiry. Coding and analyzing data depend on the researcher's theoretical position/perspective, cultural and political backgrounds, experience with the phenomenon, and knowledge of the literature. Although it is highly likely that two researchers will see similar things, interrater reliability is not a feature for judging the rigor of qualitative research (see Morse, 1997).

If reconceptualized as outlined above, the terms *validity, generalizability,* and *reliability* make sense for qualitative inquiry. This does not, however, dismiss the great thinking that has created the particular sets of criteria for qualitative inquiry (see Table 7.1). On the contrary, the reconceptualization of these terms invites, envelops, and encourages thinking courageously and creatively about criteria while boldly pursuing science. Using conventional terms encourages "being true to a world known through the empirical senses" (Richardson, 2000, p. 254), yet also freedom to attend to the ethical, moral, literary, political, critical, and creative intentions of our work. Using conventional terms also clarifies, for all scientists, how we all (working, e.g., in natural or social sciences, experimental or applied) aim to develop new knowledge and improve the human condition.

It is quite plausible to call qualitative work valid, generalizable, and reliable while adhering to the hallmark of good qualitative research: variability, not standardization (Popay, Rogers, & Williams, 1998). If nothing else, using conventional criteria diminishes the bewilderment and slight mayhem that the sets of alternative criteria evoke in new qualitative researchers.

## No Criteria

The third, unlikely option is to avoid the use of criteria altogether. Although this might be an option for more experienced and well-established researchers, it may not be viable for a doctoral student and an unrelenting supervisory committee.

## Being Rigorous

I maintain that rigor works for qualitative inquiry. Rigor does not mean, however, that you cook up the findings in your head. There is some logic to them. If someone asks, "Why did you say this or that about the phenomenon?" you are able to give a reasonable explanation. Even if you present a collage representing the experience of parents whose child committed suicide, the choice of colors and the placement of images is deliberate, meaningful, and purposeful. It tells a story. Furthermore, as the researcher, you know why it tells a story and you can answer why the color blue is used as the overall hue. It is not because your favorite color is blue.

I embrace how I am involved in my research, how I construct my research, how I generate or make data, and how I (re)present and write. I try to be reflexive. I do my best to ensure that I work with images and people's stories that help explain, in the context of a particular literature, why our world works the way it does. I think this is good research. I do not call it a game; I call it rigor.

It is important to do work that will open up people's minds. Revisit what you are trying to do in your research and make decisions, in consultation with interested and supportive others, that make sense and allow the phenomenon to be unfastened or opened up. Whether you are thinking about participatory action research, semiotics, or phenomenology, it does not matter. Do and write your research so that its integrity and rigor are apparent. Ask yourself how and why is this good science?

## Verification Strategies

It is one thing to be able to talk about rigor in qualitative inquiry; it is another to be able to share how you *do* rigor. Effective strategies that help to ensure rigor are anchored in verification. In this section I will draw heavily on the work of Morse et al. (2002).

Verification is the process of checking, confirming, disconfirming, and accounting for variability, and being certain, even if your goal is to represent uncertainty. Verification strategies include researcher responsiveness, methodological coherence, appropriate and adequate sampling, collecting and analyzing data concurrently, and thinking theoretically. These strategies, inherent in the conduct of qualitative research, help the researcher identify when to continue, stop, or modify the research to ensure rigor.

First, *researcher responsiveness* refers to the researcher's "creativity, sensitivity, flexibility and skill" (Morse et al., 2002, p. 5). This makes some quantitative as well as qualitative researchers very nervous. The notion that the researcher is an instrument for ensuring rigor is contrary to all that we have learned about objectivity. But the strength of qualitative inquiry comes from the ability of the researcher to be an analytical and critical thinker. For example, it is vital that the researcher be open to the data and "willing to relinquish any ideas that are poorly supported, regardless of the excitement and the potential that they first appear to provide" (p. 5). The lack of responsiveness of the investigator "may be due to lack of knowledge," adhering too closely to instructions or prescriptions and not listening to data, inability to abstract or get beyond the technicalities of coding, "working deductively (implicitly or explicitly)" from a theory, or "following instructions in a rote fashion" (p. 5).

Different data might demand to be treated differently, so the method, research question, or sampling plans need to be changed slightly or altogether. For example, a student was studying child sex workers in Vietnam and proposed a grounded theory to understand how they became involved in prostitution. While collecting her data, however, she described how she could not chop up her data into categories, finding a core category and basic social process. These girls spoke to her in stories, and the data demanded she stay in this form. She changed her method to narrative.

Second, attention to *methodological coherence,* as introduced in Chapter 1, will ensure congruence between your ontological and epistemological viewpoints, your theoretical position/perspective, the method you choose, your research question, and so on. If, for example, the researcher's theoretical position/perspective does not fit with the research question, rigor is compromised. For instance, a postpositivist would not produce a paper on the autoethnographic reading of Foucault (Kaufmann, 2005), and an autoethnography typically does not have a stated research question.

Third, *sampling,* as outlined in Chapter 4, must be appropriate and adequate (Morse et al., 2002). Your sample must include participants who can speak to the topic or phenomenon and can provide sufficient data to enable an in-depth and rich description of the phenomenon. Seeking negative cases is also essential to developing the analysis and seeing aspects of the phenomenon that are initially unnoticeable. If the sampling plan invites participants who do not speak in-depth to the phenomenon, your data will be thin and your findings shaky, and rigor will be jeopardized. For example, for my study on cultural competence in hospitals, I was thrilled when senior-level decision makers agreed to be interviewed. However, I learned quickly that it was important for these decision makers to support and reinforce hospital policies; the interviews sounded like a reading of the hospital policy and procedure manual. Although focusing on what they did not say would have been interesting, this was not the purpose of my study. I changed my sample to midlevel managers, those who had some decision-making power and responsibility for ensuring the practice of culturally competent care but who still worked very closely with the nurses in their day-to-day practice.

Fourth, *collecting and analyzing data concurrently*, as introduced in Chapter 6, forms a mutual interaction between what is being learned and what one needs to learn (Morse et al., 2002). Shifting back and forth between data collection and analysis allows the researcher to move with the data and learn about unique and untold aspects about the phenomenon. If all of the data are collected and analysis follows, as captured by the phrase "I have collected all my data, now I just have to analyze them," the research will not have been modified as necessary, and rigor will be compromised.

Finally, *thinking theoretically* requires working with the data from a macro-micro perspective, cautiously using the literature, and "inching forward without making cognitive leaps" (Morse et al., 2002, p. 6). If a researcher does not dwell with the data but instead leaps to conclusions after viewing the first few images or reading the first few interviews, the research is not rigorous.

For example, initial interviews with police officer participants and how they describe inner city policing might sound shocking. They refer to "drunks," "addicts," "junkies," or numbers (e.g., "This guy is 10-18," meaning "intoxicated person"). A cognitive leap might lead you to brand these police officer participants as ignorant, unprofessional, or racist/classist. Your thesis in this work is how police officer participants use language to dehumanize so that they can maintain their authoritative role. However, you recognize, after working theoretically, how these police officers understand and work on a daily basis with the social determinants of health, and have a very in-depth, complex, and problematized understanding of them. They know and experience more than many other professionals how poverty, addictions, immigrant status, lack of housing and access to health care, among other factors, are determinants of health and well-being and interact to create crime. The language they use is part of the professional discourse found in any profession (e.g., public health nurses, teachers, or social workers) that enables them to work through the most difficult situations.

Together, these five verification strategies incrementally and interactively contribute to ensure rigor. In addition, there are other well-established strategies that can be used during the research to contribute to rigor.

## Other Strategies

Returning to Lincoln and Guba (1985), some of their suggested strategies for ensuring trustworthiness include prolonged engagement, participant checks, journal writing, peer review, and audit trails.

*Prolonged engagement* is about spending a considerable amount of time in the setting to avoid making grandiose interpretations based on limited contact. The researcher, as a participant in the setting, becomes familiar with the people and the everyday situation to be able to distinguish among routines, common occurrences, and unusual events. For example, a researcher interested in the culture of a young offenders' center needs to visit more than once or twice to understand the nuances in such a setting. One visit and a subsequent write-up of the research will not produce rigorous research.

*Participant checks* is the process of obtaining feedback from participants. The researcher checks or verifies developing hypotheses and interpretations with participants (Guba & Lincoln, 1989) to determine whether they "make sense" to participants. This strategy however, becomes less useful when participants try but cannot identify their individual stories in the emerging representation or theory. Their individual stories have been joined together with others, synthesized, and abstracted into a collective story about the phenomenon. Be careful if and when you use participant checks. Early in the research process they might contribute to rigor, but later on they might jeopardize it. The only exception to this is when conducting community based or participatory action research. The nature of these approaches requires participants to be co-researchers, interpreting the data as a collective along the way.

Keeping a *personal journal* serves as a record of the researcher's assumptions, perspectives on how the research is unfolding, frustrations, challenges, and highlights. A bad day in the field might alter the way in which the researcher works with the data, and recording this is helpful when analyzing the data and for ensuring rigor. Although the journal is a source of data, it is the researcher's alone and does not have to be shared with a committee or team members. It is also separate from field notes.

*Peer review* is the process of engaging another research colleague in an extended and extensive discussion of one's process in working with the data (Morse & Field, 1995). By having a critical and supportive colleague ask questions of tentative analyses, the researcher can attend to rigor.

The *audit trail* is a documentation of "the researcher's decisions, choices, and insights" (Morse & Field, 1995, p. 144). Think about it like your tax preparation and the documents you must be able to provide to support your claims if audited. Similarly, the research audit trail enables the researcher to document why, when, and how decisions were made throughout the research process. The rationale for a decision, if left undocumented, might not make sense later in the research process. The researcher might have a difficult time building on or defending the analysis if major analytical decisions cannot be supported or recounted, which compromises rigor.

Although these well-established strategies are important for ensuring rigor, perhaps the most important strategy, which weaves throughout the entire research process, is reflexivity. Reflexivity as it relates to representation and writing is outlined in the final chapter of this book.

## Summary

I understand why some researchers embrace rigor, why others reject it, and why many are just plain confused. Qualitative research involves the hard work of checking, confirming, and reconsidering. It is not just about finding themes. It is scientific, it is thoughtful, and it provides "evidence." A light does not shine down, the heavens do not open up, and words do not fall from the sky and land on the paper. There is logic behind the decisions we make in our research. Why we excluded or included and focused on certain things all relate to rigor. Consider your options for addressing rigor. Do not shy away from questions of rigor. Instead, conduct your research and write in a way that demonstrates why your research is excellent.

# Exercise 7.1: Examining Criteria/Standards

The objective of this exercise is to become familiar with various criteria and/or standards for ensuring rigor and determine strategies that demonstrate how each can be met. This exercise is best completed in a small group.

Get into a group of four people. Each person should choose and become familiar with one set of criteria/standards for ensuring rigor in qualitative research. You may use the ones listed in Table 7.1. In a group discussion, compare and contrast the criteria/standards. Which ones are essentially the same (with different names) and which ones are unique? Among all of the criteria/standards, choose at least four that you like best and describe why. From this list, describe how each criterion/standard will be met in the process of doing your research. Argue whether you can work with these criteria /standards using the terminology of validity, reliability, and generalizability.

Chapter 8

# Proposal Writing

This chapter provides tips on preparing a qualitative proposal for funding. It is organized according to stages: Before Writing, Writing, and Coordinating the Submission.

Once I was involved in writing a letter of intent and, subsequently, a full proposal for a large national funding agency; the proposal was scored very high but was not funded. A coordinator from the funding body called the principal investigator shortly after the full proposal decisions were made to explain that we needed to tweak a few statements and to encourage us to resubmit for the same competition running again in a few months. We resubmitted, but this time did not make it beyond the letter-of-intent stage. In other words, one proposal was close to being funded, and a few months later, a resubmission for the same competition was not compelling or competitive enough to be invited for a full proposal.

Proposal writing is a bizarre enterprise. Guidelines for proposal writing can be found in many texts, on funders' Websites, and through funder-sponsored proposal-writing sessions. Another excellent source is a colleague's successful proposal. A copy of a colleague's funded proposal is a gift and you owe them if they extend such an offer. Yet the story above demonstrates that proposal writing goes beyond declared guidelines or what was funded (or close to being funded) in the past. In this chapter, I try to balance common tips on proposal writing with some specific advice on proposal writing for qualitative research.

# Before Writing: Proposals and Politics

Writing a proposal, any proposal, is a political exercise, and the proposal itself is a political document. Assessments of the value of your proposal are rooted in predominant values and power structures. Before you refine your topic and write your proposal, it is worthwhile to consider these values and power structures and how they are manifested in established research priorities, methodological favorites, and legitimate and fashionable language. Exercise 8.1 (Proposal Savvy) will help you do this. In addition, before you start writing, time needs to be spent reviewing funder and submission requirements.

## Knowing Research Priorities

Push aside your lifelong research dream of studying teaspoon disappearance (Lim, Hellard, & Aitken, 2005). Spend time, if you want to be funded, on some major funders' Websites to learn what your lifelong dream should immediately become. Our funding agencies, through periodic congresses or panel meetings, set research agendas and priorities that "formalize the boundaries of acceptable (fundable and publishable) inquiry" (Ray & Mayan, 2001, p. 58). In addition to overall research agendas, special calls periodically appear that designate circumscribed topics for investigation. Although such calls reduce fragmentation and clarify focus, certain knowledge of particular groups remains unprivileged (Ray & Mayan, 2001). What is being funded right now? Obesity research, information technology, knowledge translation, aging, pandemic preparedness, work with Aboriginal/Native American populations, and environmental research, to name a few. Although there is still money in HIV/AIDS research, this topic does not have the presence it had a decade ago. Knowing what the current research priorities are is important for choosing and narrowing your particular topic.

## Knowing Methodological Favorites

The randomized control trial (RCT) is considered to be, within the medical research community, the methodological "gold standard" against which all methods are weighed and measured. The dominance of the RCT was made apparent through an article by Smith and Pell (2003), who completed a systematic review of RCTs to determine "whether parachutes

are effective in preventing major trauma related to gravitational challenge" (p. 1459). Their conclusion reads as follows:

> As with many interventions intended to prevent ill health, the effec-
> tiveness of parachutes has not been subjected to rigorous evaluation by
> using randomised controlled trials. Advocates of evidence based medi-
> cine have criticised the adoption of interventions evaluated by using only
> observational data. We think that everyone might benefit if the most
> radical protagonists of evidence based medicine organised and partici-
> pated in a double blind, randomised, placebo controlled, crossover trial
> of the parachute. (p. 1459)

Even if you do not consider RCTs appropriate for your area of research,
the pervasive effects of this gold standard seep into our psyches and affect
proposal reviews. Clearly, to have a study funded, your method must fit
your research question. However, for qualitative research you must balance proposing creative or new research methods and data collection
strategies with more recognizable methods and conventional strategies.
Innovative or divergent methods may be marginalized when conformity
is the priority (Ray & Mayan, 2001). For example, a grounded theory with
interviews might be more recognizable and fundable than an autoethnography with personal diaries. Gauging the popularity and acceptability of
newer methods should be considered when applying for funding.

## Knowing Legitimate and Fashionable Language

Language has power, and you must use particular language, depending
on the competition and funding source. For example, a competition that
attracts traditional medical or economic models of health care requires
corresponding language of supply and demand, efficiency, effectiveness, cost benefit, minimizing risk, and health care as a commodity. In
contrast, a competition that values a collective welfare model uses language such as social solidarity, distributive justice, equity, and well-being
(Melhado, 1998). Although both models involve attempts to explain and
describe the best operation of a health care system, you should determine
which set is most legitimate for the competition.

Language use for proposal writing is also a fashion statement. Certain terms may be fashionable in one granting season and "out of date"
in the next. For example, fashionable phrases for me are currently capacity building, lifelong learning, reducing health disparities, and rural and
remote health. I no longer use empowerment. It is important to review the

request for proposals very carefully to determine the fashion for the season and deliberately, yet cautiously, insert these words into the proposal.

## Knowing the Details

After you become comfortable with the current political landscape in which your proposal will be placed, the next *step* is actually a *leap* into details. It is important to get to know details about the funder and submission requirements. This means spending time checking a funder's mission, your eligibility to apply, submission deadlines, requirements for registration (if any), rules about multiple submissions, and so on. It is also important to familiarize yourself with the format and form of proposals. Often, for trainee (student) awards the supervisor has more to complete than the trainee, so offering to help the supervisor complete her or his part will likely be accepted.

Then it is time to do an armchair walkthrough. (See Chapter 1.) Figure out what kind of question(s) you want to ask and what you want to be able to say at the end of your study. Practice speaking out loud about your proposal to whomever will listen. Hold seminars with other students. Being forced to articulate your ideas makes them clearer. Get to the point of having your proposal so well thought out that you can say, "It's all done. Now I just have to write it."

# Writing

Proposal writing is much more than an introduction, a stated research question, a method, and so on. Proposal writing is like telling a story. It is introducing the setting and characters, describing the problem, and developing the story by outlining key events (literature to date). However, at the climax or height of action, you introduce your research, demonstrating how it is necessary to resolve the problem or complete the story. This all must be done creatively and intriguingly, yet according to convention, including dealing with quantitative forms, providing the rationale, writing the literature review, detailing the methods, creating the budget, and developing plans for knowledge translation.

## Dealing with Quantitative Forms

One of the most difficult things about writing qualitative proposals is the quantitatively structured questions and form of funding applications.

For example, a section on the statement of the hypothesis and one on research outcomes are typical. Do not leave the sections blank, but answer them, educating the reviewer about qualitative work in the process. For instance, you can state that qualitative work, because of its exploratory, descriptive nature, does not have a hypothesis but relies instead on a research question to guide inquiry. For research outcomes, you may state that we do qualitative research (and you can state your particular topic) because we do not yet know what the phenomenon is, so specific outcomes cannot be determined at this point (proposal stage). However, because proposals are often heavily judged on the outcomes, or what the funder will get for its money, you must give some idea or examples of what might be produced through your study (e.g., a model, taxonomy, collage, or concept) and how this can contribute to knowledge, change practice, or influence policy. In other words, the rule for writing qualitative proposals from a quantitative form is to twist the question to make it work to your advantage.

## Providing the Rationale

Often I read in the rationale section of qualitative proposals that the study is needed because the research to date on the topic has only been quantitative. This is not a rationale. If the extant literature answers the research questions posed, so what if the research has been quantitative? The rationale should be content specific and must indicate that research to date has demonstrated "ABC about the topic," but "we do not yet know D" (an area for further research). In other words, you do not argue for the need for a qualitative method; you argue for the need for your study and fully develop this argument in your literature review. You introduce the method most appropriate for studying D (a qualitative method) in the method section.

## Writing the Literature Review

At least once a semester, a student claims that Barney Glaser recommended not writing a literature review to ensure that prior concepts and theories are not placed on the data. Although the comment is made, and visions of avoiding this tremendous task are dancing in students' heads, they know this is nonsense. You must write a literature review.

The role of the literature review is to build on the argument stated in the rationale but with more breadth, depth, and persuasion, or, as

Jan Morse (personal communication, May 12, 1999) has taught: "to get the reviewers to think as you think." The literature review provides the opportunity for you to analyze relevant prior work (including your own) for gaps and opportunities not taken to collect certain types of data or perform particular analyses. The literature review must demonstrate how your research will contribute to existing knowledge and perhaps to policy and practice.

Yet writing the literature review is a balancing act. You can reference your own work but not too much of your own work. You need to write with a sense of urgency (to communicate the importance of funding your research) yet cannot come across as fanatical or unable to appreciate others' work. You must reference current literature yet acknowledge past contributions. You must present your research as original and innovative but also demonstrate how it has developed from extant literature. (Never state that nothing has been done in the field.) Headings are extremely helpful to guide the reader, but too many make the proposal choppy. Tell the story but remind the reviewer often of the significance of the problem. Visuals are recommended, but only if they summarize and simplify the text.

Students also get sucked into the myth that you can review only qualitative literature for a qualitative proposal and only quantitative literature for a quantitative proposal. This is ridiculous. You should clearly outline and make the case for your proposed study using extant knowledge, regardless of whether it is produced through quantitative or qualitative studies. In addition, you may review other literature, including media, legal and policy documents, position papers, and so on, that can help you make your case. For example, if your topic is part of a new policy priority of a particular national or international agency, this should be included.

The literature review is also the time to "name-drop." Try to become familiar with the important scholars in the field (and with the methods they use), and then build on (not condemn) their work. If someone is particularly famous (e.g., Stephen Lewis), introduce him as such so that the significance of the statement (on HIV/AIDS in Africa) is communicated. It is best to avoid long lists of citations to try to convince funders of your knowledge in the area. Instead, try to include the author who first had the idea and then others who modified it. Finally, funders often make available the names of reviewers. Although committee members would "see through" a reference list that—surprise!—includes each member, not referencing a committee member who is somehow attached to your area is also unwise.

The literature review should also include what Sandelowski and Barroso (2003) have called strategic disarmament. This is a very helpful strategy that demonstrates your maturity as a researcher and knowledge of the field. Strategic disarmament entails anticipating and addressing "likely areas of controversy, debate, or differences of opinion" throughout the proposal, whether related to the literature, your argument, or your method (p. 782). For example, if you propose to videotape participants in their workplace (e.g., social workers counseling a client, police responding to a call, doctors performing a procedure), the likely criticism will be that participants' behavior might change as a result of being watched and, consequently, this might compromise the validity of the research (the good old Hawthorne effect). Strategic disarmament, in this case, would include referencing other studies (in the method section) in which videotaping was used that indicate how, after a time, participants usually return to typical patterns of behavior (i.e., they forget about the camera). In addition, participants "being watched" often grow to appreciate your research and will actually acknowledge and describe (in follow-up interviews) how and why the problem you are studying exists (e.g., in a study on medical error, the nurse describes how and why medicine delivery can so easily lead to error). By anticipating and directly addressing a likely criticism, reviewers will be "disarmed" and, consequently, unable to attack your proposal.

## Detailing the Methods

Years ago, we were taught to assume that reviewers would be quantitative and so would be looking for a sampling frame and operationally defined variables, and so on. We needed to write for this audience, explaining ad nauseam every step and describing why the research was different from quantitative. (This may help explain why some students provide the rationale and argue for the method instead of the topic as described above.) This has changed somewhat. Qualitative reviewers certainly exist, yet caution is still advised: Expect a review committee with strong qualitative expertise, but risk rejection if you assume as much. For example, should we have to explain why our sample sizes are small or why we do not worry about sampling bias? I have learned by attending funder proposal writing workshops and by reviewing and receiving enough rejected proposals that the most common comment made on qualitative methods sections is "not enough detail," especially of the analysis section. For that reason, when writing proposals, I can only guess what needs to be explained and what I can assume a reviewer to know.

There is one other difficulty in writing the methods section. First, you must juxtapose the need for a highly specific research plan against the iterative and emergent nature of qualitative research. However, your writing cannot be circuitous; you must write in a linear fashion. You must provide details, especially related to the way in which you will analyze your data, so that your proposal is clear and judged to be extremely well thought out. You can, however, subtly and carefully remind the reviewer that, for example, your data collection and analysis process will be reviewed after you have analyzed the initial data and will be modified, if necessary, according to the form of the data, the needs of participants, and so on.

Finally, always address rigor, and be forthright and unapologetic about the strategies you will use to ensure it (as described in Chapter 7). This is also a good place to identify official or unofficial consultants (e.g., others on campus or in the community) who can assist you in areas where you do not have experience (e.g., a new method or with a unique population) to ensure that your research is rigorous. This is also an example of strategic disarmament. And remember that the rigor of the research is not demonstrated through the use of a number of buzzwords, or what Piantanida and Garman (1999) called "The Kitchen Sink Syndrome" (p. 65). It is demonstrated through a clear research plan, described in a linear, straightforward fashion that oozes confidence, competence, and skill.

## Creating the Budget

A budget is much more than just numbers; it is an excellent conceptual summary of your research. By comparing the budget with the design, a reviewer is able to comment on your ability to organize the overall project and how carefully the proposal was prepared. For that reason, do not attempt to complete your budget just before you send in the application. Work on it on an ongoing basis so that it reflects a coherent plan for doing the research.

The greatest mistake qualitative researchers make with regard to budgets is promising considerable outcomes on a minuscule budget. You cannot bring about world peace on $10,000 over a three-year period. Although all researchers may have the tendency to underbudget their research, I think qualitative researchers fall prey to this more often than their quantitative colleagues because of our history as a marginalized methodology. We are so grateful for funding that we "promise the moon" (something impossible). Qualitative research is expensive. The costs of transcription, equipment, software, meetings, participant involvement, and so on add up quickly. Do not try to convince yourself that you will happily do all the transcription.

Different funders have varying rules on what is an allowable expense. Many do not allow or else severely restrict "hosting" costs (buying doughnuts for a focus group), transportation for participants, and if and how honoraria can be paid to participants.

If you are applying to various funders, state this in each application. This is often considered desirable as the funder can claim to support you but does not have to provide full funding.

### It Ain't Over 'til It's Over: Knowledge Translation

"It ain't over 'til it's over" is an adage to convey that anything can happen and that no one should assume the outcome of an activity or event (e.g., the final score in a football game) until it is actually over. Today, the research proposal is not over (completed) until knowledge translation (KT) has been thoroughly addressed. KT, or whichever term your funder prefers (e.g., knowledge transfer, knowledge mobilization), assumes the uptake of knowledge or the use of your findings. A proposal can no longer conclude with a promise to publish in a scholarly journal and/or present at a conference. A proposal must now include an array of strategies, ideally developed with "end users," for reaching a variety of target audiences, including research partners, communities, wider professional audiences, policymakers, and the public in general. These KT strategies include reports and presentations but also things like Websites, online learning modules, publications in street newspapers, ethnic radio presentations, dramas, art exhibits, and so on. Funders nowadays pay a great deal of attention to plans for KT, so do not assume that you have created an outstanding proposal unless this section is well done. As well, do not forget to budget (approximately 10% of the total) for KT activities.

## Coordinating the Submission

Have different people, ideally someone who knows the topic area and someone who does not, review the content of the proposal. Have a colleague or graduate student review the entire submission for completeness. Make sure to follow the guidelines impeccably (e.g., margin width, line spacing, character spacing, font, type size, page length, and referencing). Technical violations may disqualify an otherwise perfect application. Do not trust your computer spell-checker. I have read proposals that repeatedly used "police" instead of "policy," "won" instead of "own," and "pubic" instead of "public"! It is also always essential to use an editor. Attachments allowed as part of the proposal are often limited but will likely include letters, which can be letters of reference, letters of support, and letters of access. These letters are provided for different purposes, so make sure that they read differently.

*Letters of reference* are commonly required for trainee awards and for smaller, private funders. These letters should focus primarily on your strengths and abilities and assure the funder that you are competent to complete the research. Ask people who know you well (e.g., a supervisor) and who you trust to write a strong letter on your behalf. Depending on the funder and privacy laws, applicants may request, after the competition, copies of the letters of reference that were submitted on their behalf.

*Letters of support* are typically required for operating grants and convey the numerous and significant benefits that will result to a variety of groups as a result of the research. These letters, written, for example, by community members, community/not-for-profit executive directors, or hospital administrators, demonstrate how much better policy, practice, well-being, and so on will be after your research is conducted.

*Letters of access* are letters from gatekeepers. Regardless of how outstanding your proposal is, if you do not have permission to be in the community, clinic, or organization to do your study, then the proposal is for naught. These letters should simply state that you are welcome to be in the setting. If the author can provide you with space, access to documents, or something else that will make it easier for you to do your research, this should also be stated.

The final coordination of all this, especially for a large grant, should earn the applicant a certificate in project management.

## Summary

Superior proposal writing will come from the experience of writing your own proposals and from receiving your first rejections and comments from reviewers. Do not despair too long after a rejection; a rejection is not necessarily a comment on the quality of your work. There are often multiple confounding factors involved that we cannot even begin to imagine, and there are always more proposals than pots of money. Try to address the reviewers' comments and then, with renewed hope, find the next competition and try again.

# Exercise 8.1: Proposal Savvy

The objective of this exercise is to help you understand the established research priorities, methodological favorites, and legitimate and fashionable language that dominate your discipline and area of interest. This exercise is to be completed individually, with the option of bringing it to a small or large group discussion afterward.

Go to your top funders' Websites and search for their special calls, requests for proposals, and priority areas, etc. Pay attention to the description of and language used to frame these topics. Also review funders' announcements for topics, language, and methodology of recently funded proposals. In addition, ask the opinion of friendly and knowledgeable people in your discipline regarding topics, language, and methodology. Do not forget to look at private foundations. Sometimes these funders stress other priorities and allow for more creative methodological approaches. After this exercise, answer the following questions:

- What are currently the most popular topics in your area? For whom? What is and who are conspicuously missing?
- What language or sets of terms dominate in your discipline?
- What methods hold superior in your area? Are any more avant-garde approaches being considered?

After completing this individually, you may bring your answers to a small or large multidisciplinary group. Compare and contrast each member's answers and discuss any common threads within the funding context across disciplines.

## Chapter 9

# Ethics Boards, Risk, and Qualitative Research

This brief chapter addresses the limited view of ethics and our obsession of "getting through ethics." It outlines ways of understanding and minimizing risk in a qualitative project.

## Ethics: Beyond "Getting through Ethics"

**Y**our proposal for funding will contain an ethics section, in which you must either attach a certificate of approval or, more likely, state that ethics approval will be secured if and after the proposal has been funded. Ethics approval, however, requires yet another proposal. The main purpose of the ethics proposal submitted to research ethics boards (REBs) in Canada or institutional review boards (IRBs) in the United States is to outline how the rights of research participants will be respected and how participants will be protected from harm. This is done primarily through the creation of a simple, yet comprehensive, information sheet and consent form, written at an appropriate reading level, and by adhering to proper procedures to ensure that participants fully understand the research and consent (e.g., their right to withdraw at any time, refuse to answer any question, participate voluntarily). Unfortunately, however, ethics has come to mean narrowly, for many of us, "getting through ethics." We have become obsessed with the process, so much so, that once the proposal has "gone through ethics," we falsely believe that we have done our duty to ensure ethical treatment of participants.

Your obligation as a newcomer to qualitative inquiry is to understand that ethics is much, much larger than this. In doing so, you must become familiar with the issues at the intersection of ethics boards and qualitative research and how risks are understood in the context of qualitative inquiry.

## Qualitative Research and Ethics Boards

The inductive and relational nature of qualitative inquiry and "getting through ethics" often clash. For instance, qualitative ethics proposals cannot provide the amount of detail (e.g., exact sample size, precise interview questions, number of interviews per person) frequently required by ethics boards. This engenders some discomfort for boards. Moreover, discomfort escalates when qualitative researchers argue that rules for determining "what is" consent, and when and how to obtain it, can interrupt the researcher-participant relationship, are not applicable to more participatory research methods (e.g., anonymity and confidentiality), and run counter to observational research, especially research conducted in public places (van den Hoonaard, 2002).

Furthermore, a primary concern of ethics boards is the possibility that participants will become emotionally distressed as a result of participating in the research. Generally, boards target concerns toward the qualitative interview and what researchers can offer distressed participants after the interview. As long as you have counseling referral established, boards seem to be satisfied that any emotional distress will be managed (Morse, Niehaus et al., 2008), yet this is based on two questionable assumptions (as outlined by, Morse Niehaus et al., 2008). First, if distress is evident during an interview, the researcher (not a post hoc referral) is the only one who can alleviate the immediate situation. Second, distress apparent during an interview is not necessarily an abnormal response but, indeed, may be normal, given the topic being discussed (e.g., caring for a dying loved one). Ethics boards must seriously ask themselves if, for instance, crying "during the telling of one's story constitutes harm" (p. 209), or if it can actually be a benefit.

Issues such as these have been brought forward in an effort to change how members of ethics boards think about ethics and qualitative research. As a result, particular qualitative research is now exempt from some ethical review (e.g., oral history), and the argument currently exists to establish boards based on method instead of discipline (American Association of University Professors, 2006). Moreover, some researchers wish for the model followed by many European and other universities where ethics boards do not exist. Although some researchers are aghast with this apparent lack of concern and regard for the ethical conduct of research, others argue that researchers are better prepared to conduct ethical inquiry because they think about and appreciate ethics beyond "getting through ethics." Exercise 9.1 (Ethics without REBs/IRBs) addresses this issue.

To help address some of the qualitative research issues challenging ethics boards, Morse, Niehaus et al. (2008) conducted a survey of qualitative researchers to determine their perceptions of participant risk associated with qualitative interviews. They outline six overlapping ways of understanding risk: risk related to the participant, the topic, the relationship, the environment, the outcome of the research, and the researcher.

## Risks Related to the Participant

The concerns related to the participant are the conventional and well-taught risks such as true voluntary participation (i.e., not coerced through money or by a person in power, such as a physician), freedom not to answer a particular interview question, freedom to quit the research at any time, choice about how much and to what degree to disclose, and so on. In addition, risks related to the participant include participant experiences or characteristics that may make them especially vulnerable; for example, participants who have been emotionally traumatized (e.g., sexually abused), those who have been asked to speak about illegal behavior (e.g., consumer of internet pornography), those who are in the middle of a crisis (e.g., postpartum depression), those who have not resolved a crisis (e.g., the death of a loved one), and generally those who have harmed or have been harmed. The "unpredictability of the participant's emotional state" (Morse, Niehaus et al., 2008, p. 204) and the participants' potential unawareness of what upsets them until they start to articulate it increase the potential complexity of the qualitative interview.

## Risks Related to the Topic

Considering the topic is important when assessing participant risk. Topics that make participants feel vulnerable (like those listed above) and arouse feelings such as "sorrow, grief, frustration, and anger, anxiety and shame" (Morse, Niehaus et al., 2008, p. 207) can potentially make the interview more difficult for the participant. Researchers must ensure they are very comfortable discussing the research topic before engaging a participant in it.

## Risks Related to the Relationship

The research relationship has risks that are associated with control over the research relationship (and the likely power imbalance), and rest on the development of rapport, respect, and trust (Morse, Niehaus et al., 2008). However, it is misguided to think that the researcher always has the power in the research relationship. I have heard numerous examples over the years where the participant was clearly the one with more power and fully managed the inquiry (e.g., government officials, executive directors of "street" organizations, union leaders). In addition, ethicists typically warn researchers to "know your boundaries" and not become "too involved" with participants (Morse, Niehaus et al., 2008). However, what constitutes becoming too involved is debatable. Are you too involved if you write a friend's or partner's narrative as she or he dies (see Ellis, 1995; Richardson, 2007) or if you become an advocate for the issue? These relational concerns surface especially in autoethnography and community-based and/or participatory action research, where the research relationship is highly involved and does not have a definite beginning or end.

## Risks Related to the Environment

Much thought has been given in recent years to where research is conducted. Rarely do we allow researchers and participants to be in locations where risks are high. For example, researchers can rarely hold interviews in participants' homes (especially alone) or in dangerous neighborhoods, in spaces of civil disturbance or war, or under circumstances in which no one can easily find them or get a hold of them. An emotionally difficult place (e.g., a hospital where a loved one died) may also be considered a high-risk location (Morse, Niehaus et al., 2008).

## Risks Related to the Outcomes of the Research

The issue of representation (see Chapter 10) seeps into the discussion of ethics and risk; it relates to if and how writing about another can be done ethically. For example, do you publish findings that may be unpopular, damaging, or unattractive to participants, or do you publish "safe" findings to save participants' "face" or maintain honor? This issue is just beginning to surface on review board checklists.

## Risks Related to the Researcher

A shift over the years has included concerns about risks related to the researcher that include physical (e.g., as related to the environment) as well as emotional risks (e.g., being affected by the participant's story or unable to handle the sensitive nature of the topic). Researchers may also face a "dangerous" participant or a participant coming to the interview with a particular agenda (e.g., participating for the sole purpose of accessing psychological help thereafter) or unrealistic expectations (e.g., the research will result in an immediate system-wide change). It is equally important, therefore, to consider how potential risks might apply not only to the participant but also to the researcher. Indeed, a proposal in which there is no concern regarding the rights and safety of the participant can still be rejected if the board has concerns over the rights and safety of the researcher.

## Minimizing Risk

The varying risks related to the participant, the topic, the relationship, the environment, the outcomes, and the researcher, as well as the inductive and relational nature of qualitative research, demonstrate the unpredictability and emergent nature of qualitative research. As such, Morse, Niehaus et al. (2008) recommend that present-day ethics boards and qualitative researchers consider the following.

Risk assessment must be reflexive and ongoing. Risk assessment is not an a priori, one-time affair. Risk does not end once the participant signs the bottom of the consent form. The researcher must assume ongoing responsibility for risk assessment and response, whereas boards must review the discipline, preparation, and qualifications of the researcher(s), the risk inherent in the topic, and the vulnerability of the population.

Researchers must anticipate the "emotional terrain" associated with the topic. Researchers must be skilled at attending and responding to emotional responses during the interview. This can be accomplished through "relational ethical responsibilities," such as "sensitivity, respect, and authenticity" (p. 211) and a solid understanding of existing knowledge regarding the emotional nature (i.e., the terrain) of the topic.

Risk assessment, prevention, and alleviation are the continual responsibilities of the researcher. A "risk safety net" should be woven together prior to the start of the project to assist the researcher in anticipating how he or she may "ethically, respectfully, and sensitively" (p. 211) respond to participants and any difficult events or reactions.

*Researchers must pay attention to their own vulnerability and that of the research team.* Vulnerability can be physical (presence in participants' homes or unsafe neighborhoods) or emotional (devastating participants' stories). The research team includes anyone working on the project, including the transcriptionist. A means of debriefing must not only be in place but be used.

*Responsibility is first to the participant and the setting and second to the goals of the research.* Decisions must be made at all times, including those related to any publications (e.g., Web pages, reports), that maintain the confidentiality of the data and participants' anonymity (if agreed on) and honor (representation of "the other"), even if the goals of the research are compromised in the process.

Common and central to reducing risk in qualitative interviews and implementing the suggested recommendations are the preparation, competence, and experience of the researcher. Indeed, our team was once told by the head of our REB, in an urgent meeting, that he was approving our controversial study procedure because, simply put, he knew our work and trusted us. Unfortunately, although experience is a key contributor to minimizing risk, ethics boards do not formally include the experience of the team in their assessments.

## Summary

As a newcomer to qualitative research, you must do all that you can to become a well-prepared and competent qualitative researcher. For those of us who are more experienced, our task is to incorporate ethics training unique to the qualitative project in ethics and qualitative classes, conference presentations, and workshops and in various other professional development opportunities. We will then be able to shift our focus from "getting through ethics" to thinking and acting ethically within the context of our highly relational and emergent inquiry.

## Exercise 9.1: Ethics without REBs/IRBs

The objective of this exercise is to consider the best way to "train" qualitative researchers to be ethical.

You are a new professor at XYZ University where no REBs/IRBs exist. You have come from a Western university and this makes you very uncomfortable. You are not worried about your own ability to conduct ethical research, but you are worried about your new students. Describe how you would teach and work with students so that by the time they do their own independent project, you would feel comfortable without formal REB/IRB review. Argue for the value of both having and not having REBs/IRBs.

## Chapter 10

# Representation, Writing, and Reflexivity

This chapter introduces the ideas of alternative vs. conventional writing, researchers' representations of "others," and the notion of reflexivity. It is included to bring new researchers, who are unsure about these issues and just require an overview, into this terrain.

The word *ethnography* is derived from two Greek words: *ethnos,* which means "foreigner" and *graphos,* which means "writing." Ethnography, therefore, crudely means "writing about others." Representation, writing, and reflexivity are entwined concepts that grew primarily out of concerns about how ethnography—writing about others—was being conducted. The concepts made ethnographers more conscious about what they said about a particular group of people and the processes (reflexivity and writing) that were available to them to think more deliberately about how they did their research. Today, however, these concepts have created an important yet slippery slope not just for ethnographers but for all qualitative researchers.

## Representation

The issue of representation in qualitative research is concerned with the lofty generalizations that researchers make about those whom they study, otherwise known as "our findings." The issue of representation grew quickly and ever more seriously, sweeping through most of the humanities and social sciences during the late 1980s and through the 1990s, making *writing about others* quite a delicate venture. When a researcher, an authority, whose PhD voice has significant currency in our society, *writes about others,* the researcher (re)presents them. What she or he says becomes a truth, a reality, an illustration of that particular group of people. The researcher portrays but might also betray the group. The researcher might essentialize, so that the characteristics of the people written about are fixed. There is no room for variation among individuals or over time. The author asserts, for example that people of this group behave in this way and that they do so because of their culture or their condition. End of story.

I like to use Edward Said's (1978) *Orientalism* as an example of the seriousness of the issue of representation. Through his work, Said "demonstrated how academic knowledge replicated and confirmed popular stereotypes which in fundamental ways were remarkably consistent over time, and he showed how the stereotypes and structures of the orient were crucial to Western fantasies of itself as the world of enlightenment, progress and evolutionary superiority" (Marcus, 2001, p. 111).

Although the representation criticism was aimed originally at ethnography, the criticism is applicable to all research, qualitative and, I would argue, quantitative. All researchers must ask: Who are we representing in our research, and who benefits from our representations? Pillow (2003) further queries: "Are representations valid? Do they matter? ... Whose story is it—the researcher or the researched?" (pp. 175–176). It is not a crisis of representation; it is a moral problem.

I ask all of my students to ponder a line from one of the greatest classic films. While they wait for a line from "The Godfather," I refer to Stan Lee's (1962) superhero Spiderman whose dying uncle taught him "With great power there must also come—great responsibility" (see Exercise 10.1: Uncle Ben's Last Words). Although many researchers unfortunately think of themselves as superheros, I reference this line in the context of representation. The privilege and power associated with writing about a group is daunting, and it should be. Just think: You will write something about someone and publish it. It compels the sometimes cheeky question: And who do you think you are? Never hide behind the belief that, as some students have expressed about their participants, "They won't read it anyway." Some students leave research because of the overwhelming responsibility that comes with writing about another and the fear that no matter how hard they try, they will not be able to avoid ill treatment of the group. As Pillow (2003) asked, "How do I represent knowing that I can never quite get it right?" (p. 176).

Yet we cannot be paralyzed when putting pen to paper. We should be engaging in research involving participants who want representation. Good research can and is being done to move us from static places. How can we best proceed? At least two options are available: writing and reflexivity.

# Writing

When learning to write, qualitative researchers should take a field trip to the children's section of a bookstore. Children's books are visually magnificent, written simply, and multisensory. There are light-up, pop-up, peek-a-boo, and folding books where images rise off the page or hide behind flaps. Some are scratch-and-sniff books: Scratch a jug of lemonade and it smells like lemons. Buttons are pressed to hear a cow moo or a train chug. Children can pet the fuzzy lion or scratch the steel wool crocodile. We want our children to learn a story through sight, smell, sound, and touch. As we leave the children's section and move into young readers, youth, and, eventually, the adult section, however, the colors, smells, sounds, and touch are gone, replaced with black-and-white printed text.

Allaying your fears concerning the issue of representation or the paralysis of putting pen to paper can start with the visit to the children's section of the bookstore and the endless possibilities of text. If qualitative researchers, in representing a group, want to share various perspectives, to open up rather than foreclose possibilities, then variations in text must be considered. A conventional format is not the only way in which knowledge can appear. Qualitative researchers can draw on and/ or produce plays, poems, films, hypermedia, cartoons, magazines, newspapers, documentaries, and fiction, to name a few. Fonts can be changed to differentiate various positions, and texts can be skirted, layered, or pleated. The possibilities available to us through experimental writing, as the name suggests, enables representation of various and diverse perspectives to be autonomous yet combined.

In representing diverse perspectives, the researcher must consider how much of her or his own voice to include. The question is no longer: Do I influence the setting, the participants, the research, and so on? You do. The question is also no longer: How do I influence the setting, the participants, the research, and so on? Qualitative research is not unidirectional; it is relational. It is an act of engagement. The researcher affects the setting and the setting affects the researcher. Through an engaged process, the researcher deliberately, more or less, attends to her or his "self" as part of the research process. It is beyond accounting for your background or what interested you in the topic. It is about how much you explicitly draw on and include your experience as data and in the representation of the findings. Making explicit the self in the research, thus creating a co-produced story or text, removes some of the fear of representing others.

The language you use when creating the text, along with experimental writing and the inclusion of self, can also address the concern with representation. The language you choose will communicate something about the stability or permanence you believe your "findings" to have. The word *findings* itself relates a sense of discovery, of claiming a newfound knowledge that was unavailable until the author's particular research was conducted and revealed it. Many qualitative researchers are now much more tentative in their claims and often present in one text numerous perspectives and possibilities and, thus, not only one story but intertwining and sometimes contradictory stories. Claims can be challenged by the researcher her- or himself. Writing with some tentativeness and impermanence removes some of the issues of representation as you leave room for the group to change or refute your account.

Overall, writing in unconventional formats, including writing the self into the research process, and presenting findings as important yet impermanent help decentralize the researcher's authority. When the researcher does so, texts are able to move around and richly communicate inherent ambiguities and various realities and positions. Indeed, "writing is not an innocent practice" (Denzin, 1999, p. 568), and regardless of what and how you write, there are few things as influential as a written text. Again, with great power comes great responsibility.

## Reflexivity

"The terms reflexive, reflexivity, and reflexiveness have been used in a variety of disciplines to describe the capacity of language and of thought—of any system of signification—to turn or bend back upon itself, to become an object to itself, and to refer to itself" (Babcock, 1980, p. 2). Barbara Babcock wrote this as the editor of a special issue of *Semiotica* to capture various philosophical critiques of positivism. Since then, reflexivity has been given a great deal of attention as fundamental to the qualitative research process, yet *what it is* or *how you do it* and, better yet, *whether it is even possible to do* are all outstanding questions in the dialogic discussions on reflexivity. In this context, Pillow (2003) remarked on this nebulous concept of reflexivity "as if it is something we all commonly understand and accept as standard methodological practice for critical qualitative research" (p. 176).

The issue of reflexivity has been in the literature since the turn of the century but became more accessible through the translations completed during the 1960s of works by, for example, Merleau-Ponty (1964), Wittgenstein (1969), and Schutz (1967). Although these authors contributed to the philosophical foundation of reflexivity, reflexivity became a broader methodological concern in the 1980s during the transition between author-evacuated, realist ethnographic texts and more mindful, transparent, and constructed ethnographic texts. Van Maanen (1988) proposed a genre of ethnography labeled *confessional ethnography,* which captures the fieldworker's trials and tribulations in which the research process becomes the focus of the ethnographic text. Hints of this form of ethnography can be found as appendices in some older ethnographies, such as Liebow's (1967) *Tally's Corner* and as full text in Rabinow's (1977) *Reflections on Fieldwork in Morocco.* Unfortunately, the intent of confessional ethnography was lost when it was engulfed by the reflexivity literature and transformed into texts that read, "I am sorry for being who I am and for seeing and working with the data the way I did; please forgive me," and, as a result of this admission, the researcher was absolved of any wrongdoing. This confessional process became a measurement of validity, a tool for enhancing objectivity, and a pander to modernity. In other words, if we can duly understand and establish how we are in the data, the data will be correct and the conclusions accurate. This is an ignorant view of confessional ethnography, an extremely limited view of reflexivity, and an unacceptable view in postmodern/poststructuralist times.

Evolving from this confessional tale, other forms of reflexivity were introduced that compelled scholars to create typologies, inventories, and other categorizations to try to capture *what it is* (see Clough, 1994; Marcus, 1994; Wilkinson, 1988; and Woolgar, 1988). Finlay (2002) has defined reflexivity as "thoughtful, conscious self-awareness" that "encompasses continual evaluation of subjective responses, intersubjective dynamics, and the research process itself" (p. 532). As Hertz (1997) described, "to be reflexive is to have an ongoing conversation about the experience while simultaneously living in the moment" (cited in Finlay, 2002, p. 532). Reflexivity is the process of being highly attentive to how and why you make decisions and interpretations along the research way, critically examining your personal-researcher role and how this interfaces with all—even the most minute—aspects of the research.

Yet we have to think very carefully about *how to do* reflexivity. Lynch (2000) has stated that although researchers trumpet the importance of reflexivity and state that they have "done it," they rarely provide any narrative outlining the process, making it "difficult to establish just what is being claimed" (p. 26). As Pillow admitted (2003), "I do remain puzzled by how to teach students how to be reflexive" (p. 177).

But before we try to figure out how to do it, we should be aware that scholars have questioned whether reflexivity is even possible. In other words, how we can be both the gazer and, at the same moment, the one gazed at? (Davies et al., 2004) Reflexivity is paradoxical as "turning in on oneself in a critical manner tends to produce awareness that there are no absolute distinctions between ... the 'self' and 'other'" (Foley, 2002, p. 473). Davis et al. have written that the reflexive process is like "being held within a hall of mirrors" (p. 386). "Standing in front of one mirror, our reflection is caught in another, and that other reflects yet another image in a ceaseless infinite regression" (p. 386). "How are we to conduct our reflexive work if the one who gazes and the one who is sometimes gazed at are themselves being constituted in the very moment of the act of gazing by discursive and political and contextual features constituting the moment of reflexivity?" (p. 368). Spivak (1991), too, has warned that our "practice is a broken and uneven place ... heavily inscribed with habit and sedimented understandings" (cited in Lather, 1993, p. 674).

The limits of our consciousness and our ability to be reflexive, as proposed by some scholars, collide with the notions of others, who wonder what the reflexivity fuss is all about. These scholars believe that we are by nature reflexive beings and that reflexivity is that which makes us human. In other words, as thinking beings we all practice some form of reflexivity (Foley, 2002). Reflexivity "is an unavoidable feature of the way actions (including actions performed, and expressions written, by academic researchers) are performed, made sense of and incorporated into social settings" (Lynch, 2000, pp. 26–27). These scholars generally consider reflexivity to be an "academic fad" (Patai, 1994, p. 64) associated with navel gazing, pretentiousness, self-indulgence, and narcissism.

Where does this leave us well-intentioned, thoughtful qualitative researchers? The questioning has not made reflexivity superfluous, nor has it dampened the reflexivity enterprise. Although it is truly impossible to "nail down" self-awareness in the hall of discursive, political, and contextual mirrors, it is important not to lose the point of reflexivity. Reflexivity needs to be about grappling with self-awareness and politics, and how we frame reality, as we conduct our research and as we write. This is not a process of "looking harder or more closely, but of seeing what frames our seeing—spaces of constructed visibility and incitements to see which constitute power/knowledge" (Lather 1993, p. 675).

Research is never undirected. Research is not free-standing. There are many possible agendas; it is important to know yours and what consistently constitutes it. It is important to seek to know but at the same time situate this knowing as tenuous (Pillow, 2003). This is the point of reflexivity.

Let us return to writing. You have drawn on the literature and called on your most beloved theorist to problematize or explain your data in the most sophisticated yet simple way. You have made your contribution to build knowledge, provide insight, instill appreciation, solve "the problem," and/or make change. Do not be disappointed in yourself if you write a conventional article; you need to reach the reader. Do not be worried if you are still puzzled about reflexivity; there is no reflexivity checklist to ensure that you did it "right." Do not be concerned if you do not think you had "an ongoing conversation about the experience while simultaneously living in the moment" (Hertz, 1997; cited in Finlay, 2002, p. 532); as you mature as a qualitative researcher, you will be able to think more about these processes. The bottom line is that you cannot become complacent.

# Summary

Can we ever, in good conscience, write anything about anyone anymore? It is a slippery slope indeed, yet it is important to remind ourselves of the spirit of qualitative inquiry. Qualitative inquiry demands the relational, the dialogic, and an understanding that our research is not "a final statement of who the research participants are, but as one move in a continuing dialogue through which those participants will continue to form themselves, as they continue to become who they may yet be" (Frank, 2005, p. 967). Qualitative research insists—thank goodness—that we can never adequately describe the human condition (Frank, 2005). In the end, we can construct sensible, complex, fascinating, and indefinite accounts of reality that simultaneously evoke wonderment and unease about what it means to be part of our social world.

# Exercise 10.1: Uncle Ben's Last Words

The objective of this exercise is to consider the extraordinary power researchers have to create knowledge and a reality about particular issues and groups. This exercise is best suited for a small group.

Peter Parker's dying uncle Ben spoke these last words to him: "With great power there must also come—great responsibility." Discuss Uncle Ben's words within the context of representation and within each member's area of research. Discuss the following questions:

- What can you do during the research process that may help with the issue of representation?

- How can you write or produce findings that may help with the issue of representation?

- What is the difference between engaging in research that may be difficult to do because of issues of representation versus not doing the research at all?

# Appendix A

# Transcription Example

Participant #03
Interview #02
Drop-in center; January 28, 2008
Interviewer #2
p.1

## Key

| P | Participant |
|---|---|
| I | Interviewer |
| \<laughter> | Laughter while speaking or after talk |
| \<crying> | Crying while speaking or after talk |
| \<other emotion> | Another emotion while speaking or talking |
| #you're# believable | Uncertain hearing (words) |
| pseudograph (fake name or place) | ~Maria |
| Real name or place | Maria |
| \<VOX> words \<VOX> | Words of another person, usually an interruption |
| .. | 2 dots – short pause |
| ... | 3 dots – long pause |
| (word inside) | Transcriber's possible hearing of the word |
| WORD | Louder/emphasized word more than normal |
| word | Softer word than normal |

BASED ON DU BOIS ET AL., 1993.

1          Participant #03

2          Interview #02

3          Drop-in center; January 28, 2008

4          Interviewer #2

5          p. 2

6

7   I: So, Janice, what is going on with you?

8

9   P: Well, like I've told child welfare that I want—Brittany to have a

10  youth worker. But, I don't want a youth worker for 3 to 6 months and

11  then they rip her— that person out of her life because that's not what

12  she needs. Sheneeds somebody long-term where that's going to be

13  there for her on a like on a continuous basis for however long she

14  needs it. Three to six months—to build a relationship with

15  somebody and then rip them out of her life is not –no# makes#

16  things worse. But they don't. <crying>

17

18  <VOX>Oh, excuse me, when will you be out of here <VOX>

19

20  P:   It's really tough though because the fact that if you don't have a

21  case open with child welfare you get nothing. They don't support

22  whatsoever and they're not willing—and they're not willing to keep

23  ongoing support. It's we're there short-term and then you're done.

24                     Participant #03

23                     Interview #02

24                     Drop-in center; January 28, 2008

25                     Interviewer #2

26                     p. 3

27

28    I:    Is it (funding)? Is that what the problem is?

29

30    I:    Yeah # talk about that because Maria's gonna try—we're

31    gonna try to tally up some key messages to send out to decision

32    makers.

33

34    P:    That was another thing too that I had to go through.

35    When I called child welfare to ask for support I told them I

36    wanted family counseling and I wanted these things. She says

37    we can't give you that on family support. She says the only

38    way we can fund that is if we have a supervision order. I SAYS

39    WELL GET ME THE DAMN SUPERVISION ORDER THEN.

40    So I have to blacken my name in order to get the support that I

41    needed and that's exactly what I did.

42

43

44

Appendix B

# Field Notes Example

## First visit to the "Center"

### June 19, 2007 (duration 7 P.M.–10:15 P.M.)

*[Note: I had been invited to a summer barbeque party same night but declined in order to go to the Meeting. When I told my prospective host what I was doing she became very upset. She told me that she had known someone who had gotten involved with this group and that they were "creepy". I was taken-a-back by her anger...I'm writing this because my sense is that this leader doesn't have the best reputation with non-congregants here]*
*[public perception]*

[Arrived at 7 P.M.—late and frustrated because I got lost. I *thought* I was late but things ended up starting later. A large group of people were waiting outside. I asked a person directing traffic why we were being put in separate lines. (Apparently, people are admitted in order according to the first letter of their first name. It rotates, giving everyone the opportunity to go in first and get a good seat.)]

[**Q:** Note to ask when their "training center" is officially opening. Also ask about Leader's schedule]

**[Description of setting]**
The Center is located on an industrial parkway—away from downtown. It is a large building—industrial looking—unremarkable and gray boxy. Once inside, I was instructed to take off my shoes and enter a large hall set up with rather nice chairs. At the back is a shop of sorts selling tapes, books, and photos of the leader. A large fish tank was located near the main entrance.

At the front of the room was a podium, an office chair—a nice table and ikebana arrangement and tall floor plant. In front hanging from the ceiling were two rotating cameras which filmed the proceedings. At the far side of the room was a recording table where two people did the tech work.

As it was my first time visiting the Center, I was told I could go right in and get a seat up front. [newcomer advantage]. I sat third from the front—behind a number of people already seated on the floor in front of the chairs.

The participants were quite attractive looking—well dressed—fairly evenly split in terms of gender. There were a few children and young teens (who sat or played quietly throughout the service) There are approx. 250 people. The atmosphere was very hushed.

> [C: This was characteristic of the entire evening. Before the questioning started, talking was kept to a minimum – hushed. Even children played at the back very quietly.]

A woman—early 40s—sat beside me. I noticed many had brought shawls, water, notebooks, and footstools. Two younger women (sisters) sat to my left. I spoke with the woman to my right (Sarah)—mostly chit-chat about living here. I asked her what I should expect—she told me that people will request to ask questions. Their name will appear on the running screen above the main stage and then they can go to a seat up front where a microphone was set up and they can ask their question to the Leader. [q & a format]

She recommended I go to a documentary playing at the local repertoire cinema [check into this film] I didn't get a chance to ask why she had suggested this film. She told me that she had just moved (I didn't ask but suspected that she had moved to be nearer to the Leader.

From a door at the front side of the hall, the Leader entered. Tall, lean, handsome—long black hair tied back in a pony tail. Ivory silk shirt, ivory slacks. He moved slowly, calmly and still. Sat at the front and looked out with a blank expression. For several minutes—maybe ten—he sat, we sat and all was quiet.

> [Those in audience didn't seem put off by this long silence – must be part of the scene.
>
> My back is already killing me.]

[Others in the audience are taking notes, so I opening record my observations in a small notebook]

*[M: Note to be prepared for all possibilities – I only brought a tiny note book when I could have written more extensive notes had a brought a larger note book.]*

Then a young girl (11–14 years—long blond hair, very thin, wearing a T-shirt that said, "drama queen") was first up to the mike. She spoke slowly, with measured speech—she spoke about a recent change in her family and how this had disrupted her life. She spoke at length about how she was observing this change and disruption—how it upset her and she does not understand and yet sometimes she does understand that with

*[AN: This is a theme that seems to run through the whole session – I don't know if it's me, but this partial understanding seems to be part of the gig here.]*

change—it is difficult, but also good—"like being able to be here with you." How change is both painful and good, and how she understands and doesn't understand. She repeated this. How she is very different from others in her school and how this is difficult but she "understands."

*[This is the theme of her commentary - she does not ask a question and the Leader does not answer – but continues to sit silently looking ahead - not at anyone in the room]*

Next to the mike was a woman in her mid 40s—Eastern European accent—small—curly brown, long hair tied back in a pony tail. She asked if the Leader could "help" her with her persistent "self-delusion."

**The Leader**—"How have I *not* helped you?"

She said she did not understand and the Leader repeated himself. "How have I *not* helped you?" She thanked him and left the seat. [Attributive wisdom]

*[AN – develop this notion of Attributive wisdom. From vague utterances, meaning is derived. Direct and explicit explanations of statements are not given.]*

The next person in the seat was a woman—early 50s—shaking (either from nervousness, or possibly Parkinson's [?]—rocking back and forth—nodding her head throughout)

She told him that the last time she had heard him speak she felt filled with the love he had for them—awash with his love and she wanted to thank him for that. She also wanted to know how to sustain that feeling of love—that after that experience she felt love for others, even her enemies. But it didn't last and she wanted to know how to make it last. [devotion]

**Leader:** "You don't need to love your enemies. You don't need enemies." [Leader speaks in a measured, monotone voice—slow, almost hesitant—but certain]

I leave. My back was killing me. I ask what the time of the next meeting—Sunday at 1–3 P.M. I don't think I can make it.

[Note to read website … next time, bring money for books—that back of the Center is a large table with photos of the Leader, and his many, many books, and [oddly enough] audio recordings of previous "talks"]

# Document Analysis Template

## Document Analysis Worksheet

| 1. | Name/title of document |
|---|---|
| 2. | Type of document (e.g., journal article, newspaper article, advertisement) |
| 3. | Date of document |
| 4. | If an edition of a document, explain |
| 5. | Author/creator(s) of document |
| 6. | Position/organization(s) of author/creator(s) |
| 7. | Background of author/creator(s) (e.g., credentials, faculty, experience) |

| 8. | General overview of the document (brief, broad perspective) |
|---|---|
| 9. | Unique characteristics of the document (does anything stand out?) |
| 10. | Tone/mood of the document (what feelings does the document stimulate?) |
| 11. | Audience for which the document was written (e.g., public, specific to organization, colleagues) |
| 12. | Language of document (e.g., research, medical, layman) |
| 13. | Patterns within the document (e.g., style, paragraphing, numbering) |
| 14. | Symbols, diagrams, pictures, visuals in document (e.g., logos, photos) |
| 15. | Viewpoint from which the document was written (may not only be the author's) |

| 16. | Purpose/objective of document (e.g., to convince, provide information) |
|-----|------------------------------------------------------------------------|
| 17. | Topic/issue of document |
| 18. | Description topic/issue in the document |
| 19. | Consistency of definitions & objectives with relation to other documents |
| 20. | Conflict or agreement with other documents about the topic/issue |
| 21. | Question(s) left unanswered by the document |

Additional Notes:

# Notes

## Chapter 1

1. Enhancing Qualitative Understanding of Illness Processes and Prevention, funded by the Canadian Institutes of Health Research.
2. This part of our conversation was written up by my colleague, Sarah Wall.
3. I thank Emily Huddart-Kennedy for her ideas on this topic.

## Chapter 2

4. Denzin and Lincoln (2005) consider the four major paradigms in qualitative inquiry to be positivist and postpositivist, constructivist-interpretive, critical, and feminist-poststructuralist.

## Chapter 3

5. An example of using a gerund would be calling a category Learning to Live Again rather than The Will to Live Again.

## Chapter 5

6. Lynn Eldershaw is an assistant professor, Department of Psychology, Social Work and Criminal Justice, University of Maine at Presque Isle.

# References

Agar, M. (2004). Know when to hold 'em, know when to fold 'em: Qualitative thinking outside the university. *Qualitative Health Research, 14*, 100–112.

Agar, M. (2006). Culture: Can you take it anywhere? *International Journal of Qualitative Methods, 5*(2), Article 11. Available online at http://www.ualberta.ca/~iiqm/backissues/5_2/HTML/agar.htm (retrieved January 17, 2008).

Agar, M., & Kozel, N. J. (1999). Introduction. *Substance Use and Misuse, 34*(14), 1936.

American Association of University Professors (AAUP). (2006). *Research and human subjects: Academic freedom and the institutional review boards.* Available online at http://www.aaup.org/AAUP/comm/rep/A/humansubs.htm (retrieved August 18, 2008).

Applegate, M., & Morse, J. M. (1994). Personal privacy and interaction patterns in a nursing home. *Journal of Aging Studies, 8*(4), 413–434.

Atkinson, R. (1997). *The life story interview.* Thousand Oaks, CA: Sage.

Atkinson, P., & Coffey, A. (2002). Revisiting the relationship between participant observation and interviewing. In J. F. Gubrium & J. A. Holstein (Eds.), *Handbook of interview research* (pp. 801–814). Thousand Oaks, CA: Sage

Atkinson, P., Coffey, A., Delamont, S., Lofland, J., & Lofland, L. (2001). Editorial introduction. In P. Atkinson, A. Coffey, S. Delamont, J. Lofland, & L. Lofland (Eds.), *Handbook of ethnography* (pp. 1–7). Thousand Oaks, CA: Sage.

Austin, W., Rankel, M., Kagan, L., Bergum, V., & Lemermeyer, G. (2005). To stay or to go, to speak or stay silent, to act or not to act: Moral distress as experienced by psychologists. *Ethics and Behavior, 15*(3), 197–212.

Babcock, B. (1980). Reflexivity: Definitions and discriminations. *Semiotica, 30* (1/2), 1–14.

Ball, M., & Smith, G. (2007). Technologies of realism?: Ethnographic uses of photography and film. In P. Atkinson, A. Coffey, S. Delamont, J. Lofland, & L. Lofland (Eds.), *Handbook of ethnography* (pp. 302–320). Los Angeles: Sage.

Ballinger, C. (2006). Demonstrating rigour and quality? In L. Finlay & C. Ballinger (Eds.), *Qualitative research for allied health professionals: Challenging choices* (pp. 235–246). Chichester, UK: John Wiley.

Banks, M. (2001). *Visual methods in social research.* London: Sage.

Barbour, R. S., & Kitzinger, J. (Eds.). (1999). *Developing focus group research: Politics, theory and practice.* Thousand Oaks, CA: Sage.

Barthes, R. (1972). *Mythologies.* (A. Lavers, Trans). New York: Hill and Wang. (Original work published in 1957.)

Bauman, Z. (2007). *Consuming life.* Cambridge, MA: Polity.

Bell, N., & Campbell, M. (2003). A child's death: Lessons from health care providers' texts. *Journal of Sociology and Social Welfare, 30*(1), 113–126.

Bernard, H. R. (2000). *Social research methods: Qualitative and quantitative approaches.* Thousand Oaks, CA: Sage.

Bloor, M., Frankland, J., Thomas, M., & Robson, K. (2001). *Focus groups in social research.* Thousand Oaks, CA: Sage.

Bochner, A. P. (2001). Narrative's virtues. *Qualitative Inquiry, 7*(2), 131–156.

Bosio, A. C., Graffigna, G., & Lozza, E. (2008). Online focus groups: Towards a theory of technique. In T. Hansson (Ed.), *Handbook of digital information technologies: Innovations and ethical issues* (pp. 192–212). Hershey, PA: Idea Group.

Brink, P. (1991). Issues of reliability and validity. In J. Morse (Ed.), *Qualitative nursing research: A contemporary dialogue* (pp. 164–186). London: Sage.

Brinkmann, S. (2007). Could interviews be epistemic?: An alternative to qualitative opinion-polling. *Qualitative Inquiry, 13*(8), 1116–1138.

Burke, K. (1969). *A grammar of motives.* Berkeley: University of California Press.

Caelli, K., Ray, L., & Mill, J. (2003). "Clear as mud": Toward greater clarity in generic qualitative research. *International Journal of Qualitative Methods, 2*(2). Article 1. Available online at http://www.ualberta.ca/~iiqm/ backissues/2_2/html/caellietal.htm (retrieved August 12, 2008).

Campbell, M., & Gregor, F. (2002). *Mapping social relations: A primer in doing institutional ethnography.* Aurora, Canada: Garamond.

Candida Smith, R. (2003). Analytic strategies for oral history interviews. In J. Gubrium & J. Holstein (Eds.), *Postmodern interviewing* (pp. 347–367). Thousand Oaks, CA: Sage.

Chaplin, E. (1994). *Sociology and visual representations.* London: Routledge.

Charmaz, K. (2000). Grounded theory: Objectivist and constructivist methods. In N. K. Denzin & Y. S. Lincoln (Eds.), *The Sage handbook of qualitative research* (2nd ed., pp. 509–536). Thousand Oaks, CA: Sage.

Charmaz, K. (2006). *Constructing grounded theory: A practical guide through qualitative analysis.* London: Sage.

Cheek, J. (1997). (Con)textualizing toxic shock syndrome: Selected media representations of the emergence of a health phenomenon 1979–1995. *Health, 1*(2), 183–203.

Clarke, A. E. (2005). *Situational analysis: Grounded theory after the postmodern turn.* Thousand Oaks, CA: Sage.

Clough, P. T. (1994). *Feminist thought: Desire, power and academic discourse.* Cambridge, MA: Blackwell.

Crush, J. (1994). Post-colonialism, de-colonization, and geography. In A. Godlewska & N. Smith (Eds.), *Geography and empire* (pp. 333–350). Oxford, UK: Blackwell.

Davies, B., Browne, J., Gannon, S., Honan, E., Laws, C., Mueller-Rockstroh, B., & Bendix, E. (2004). The ambivalent practices of reflexivity. *Qualitative Inquiry, 10*(3), 360–389.

Davies, B., Browne, J., Gannon, S., Honan, E., & Somerville, M. J. (2006). "Truly wild things": Interruptions to the disciplinary regimes of neo-liberalism in (female) academic work. In B. Davies & S. Gannon (Eds.), *Doing collective biography* (pp. 79–87). Maidenhead, UK: Open University Press.

Davies, B., & Gannon, S. (2006). The practices of collective biography. In B. Davies & S. Gannon (Eds.), *Doing collective biography* (pp. 1–15). Maidenhead, UK: Open University Press.

Debbink, G., & Ornelas, A. (1997). Cows for campesinos. In S. E. Smith, D. G. Willms, & N. A. Johnson (Eds.), *Nurtured by knowledge: Learning to do participatory action research* (pp. 13–33). Ottawa, Canada: International Development Research Centre.

Denzin, N. K. (1999). Two-stepping in the '90s. *Qualitative Inquiry, 5*, 568–572.

Denzin, N. K., & Lincoln, Y. S. (2005). Preface. In N. K. Denzin & Y. S. Lincoln (Eds.), *The Sage handbook of qualitative research* (3rd ed., pp. ix–xix). Thousand Oaks, CA: Sage.

Du Bois, J. W., Scheutze-Coburn, S., Cumming, S., & Paolino, D. (1993) Outline of discourse transcription. In J. A. Edwards & M. D. Lambert (Eds.), *Talking data: Transcription and coding in discourse research* (pp. 45–89). Hillsdale, NJ: Lawrence Erlbaum.

Duneier, M. (1999). *Sidewalk.* New York: Farrar, Straus and Giroux.

Eisenhart, M. A., & Howe, K. R. (1992). Validity in qualitative research. In M. D. LeCompte, W. L. Millroy, & J. Preissle (Eds.), *Handbook of qualitative research in education* (pp. 643–680). San Diego, CA: Academic Press.

Ellis, C. (1995). *Final negotiations: A story of love, loss, and chronic illness.* Philadelphia, PA: Temple University Press.

Ellis, C. (2004). *The ethnographic I: A methodological novel about autoethnography.* Walnut Creek, CA: AltaMira.

Ellis, C., & Bochner, A. P. (Eds.). (1996). *Composing ethnography: Alternative forms of qualitative writing.* Walnut Creek, CA: AltaMira.

Ellis, C., & Bochner, A. P. (2000). Autoethnography, personal narrative, reflexivity: Researcher as subject. In N. K. Denzin & Y. S. Lincoln (Eds.), *The Sage handbook of qualitative research* (2nd ed., pp. 733–768). Thousand Oaks, CA: Sage.

Emme, M. J. (in press). Photonovella and photovoice. In L. M. Given (Ed.), *The Sage encyclopedia of qualitative research methods.* Thousand Oaks, CA: Sage.

Emme, M. J., Kirova, A., Kamau, O., & Kosanovich, S. (2006). Ensemble research: A means for immigrant children to explore peer relationships through fotonovela. *Alberta Journal of Education Research, 52*(3), 160–181.

Fine, G. A. (1993). Ten lies of ethnography: Moral dilemmas of field research. *Journal of Contemporary Ethnography, 22*(3), 267–294.

Finlay, L. (2002). Outing the researcher: The provenance, process, and practice of reflexivity. *Qualitative Health Research, 12,* 531–545.

Finlay, L. (2006). "Rigour," "ethical integrity," or "artistry"?: Reflexively reviewing criteria for evaluating qualitative research. *British Journal of Occupational Therapy, 69*(7), 319–326.

Foley, D. (2002). Critical ethnography: The reflexive turn. *International Journal of Qualitative Studies in Education, 20,* 469–490.

Fontana, A., & Frey, J. (2005). The interview: From neutral stance to political involvement. In N. K. Denzin & Y. S. Lincoln (Eds.), *The Sage handbook of qualitative research* (3rd ed., pp. 695–728). Thousand Oaks, CA: Sage.

Fontana, A., & Prokos, A. H. (2007). *The interview from formal to postmodern.* Walnut Creek, CA: Left Coast Press.

Foucault, M. (1990). *The history of sexuality* (Vol. 1, Random House, Trans). New York: Vintage. (Original work translated in 1978.)

Foucault, M. (1998). *Aesthetics, method, and epistemology* (J. D. Faubion, Ed.). New York: The New Press.

Frank, A. W. (1995). *The wounded storyteller.* Chicago: University of Chicago Press.

Frank, A. W. (2005). What is dialogical research and why should we do it? *Qualitative Health Research, 15*, 964–974.

Freire, P. (1997). Foreword. In S. E. Smith, D. G. Willms, & N. A. Johnson (Eds.), *Nurtured by knowledge: Learning to do participatory action research* (pp. xi–xii). New York: Apex.

Garfinkel, H. (1967). *Studies in ethnomethodology.* Englewood Cliffs, NJ: Prentice-Hall.

Gee, J. P. (1991). A linguistic approach to narrative. *Journal of Narrative and Life History, 1*, 15–39.

Glaser, B. G., & Strauss, A. L. (1967). *The discovery of grounded theory: Strategies for qualitative research.* Chicago: Aldine.

Goodman, S. (2007). Piercing the veil: The marginalization of midwives in the United States. *Social Science & Medicine, 65*, 610–621.

Graffigna, G., & Bosio, C. (2006). The influence of setting on findings produced in qualitative health research: A comparison between face-to-face and online discussion groups about HIV/AIDS. *International Journal of Qualitative Methods, 5*(3), Article 5. Available online at http://www.ualberta.ca/~iiqm/backissues/5_3/PDF/graffigna.pdf (retrieved February 9, 2008).

Green J., & Hart, L. (1999). The impact of context on data. In R. S. Barbour & J. Kitzinger (Eds.), *Developing focus group research: Politics, theory and practice* (pp. 21–35). Thousand Oaks, CA: Sage.

Greenbaum, T. (1998). *The handbook for focus group research* (2nd ed.). Thousand Oaks, CA: Sage.

Guba, E. G. (1990). The alternative paradigm dialog. In E. G. Guba (Ed.), *The paradigm dialog* (pp. 17–30). Newbury Park, CA: Sage.

Guba, E. G., & Lincoln, Y. S. (1981). *Effective evaluation: Improving the usefulness of evaluation results through responsive and naturalistic approaches.* San Francisco: Jossey-Bass.

Guba, E. G., & Lincoln, Y. S. (1989). *Fourth generation evaluation.* Newbury Park, CA: Sage.

Guba, E. G., & Lincoln, Y. S. (1994). Competing paradigms in qualitative research. In N. K. Denzin & Y. S. Lincoln (Eds.), *The Sage handbook of qualitative research* (2nd ed., pp. 105–117). Thousand Oaks, CA: Sage.

Gubrium, J., & Holstein, J. (2003). (Eds.). *Postmodern interviewing.* Thousand Oaks, CA: Sage.

Gunzenhauser, M. G. (2006). A moral epistemology if knowing subjects. *Qualitative Inquiry, 12*(3), 621–647.

Harding, S. (1987). Is there a feminist method? In S. Harding (Ed.), *Feminism and methodology* (pp. 1–14). Bloomington: Indiana University Press.

Harris, K. (1995). *Collected quotes from Albert Einstein.* Available online at http://rescomp.stanford.edu/~cheshire/EinsteinQuotes.html (retrieved June 1, 2008).

Haug, F., Andersen, S., Bünz-Elfferding, A., Hauser, K., Lang, U., Laudan, M., Lüdenmann, M., Meir, U., Nemitz, B., Niehoff, E., Prinz, R., Rathzel, N., Scheu, M. & Thomas, C. (Eds.). (1987). *Female sexualization: A collective work of memory* (E. Carter, Trans.). London: Verso Press.

Have, P. ten (1998). *Doing conversation analysis: A practical guide.* Thousand Oaks, CA: Sage.

Hertzman, C., MacLean, S., Kohen, D., Dunn, J. R., & Evans, T. (2002). *Early development in Vancouver: Report of the Community Asset Mapping Project (CAMP).* Vancouver, Canada: Human Early Learning Partnership. Available online at http://ecdportal.help.ubc.ca/pubMaps/camp/vancouverreport.pdf (retrieved May 11, 2008).

Hodges, A. (2007). The political economy of truth in the "war on terror" discourse: Competing visions of an Iraq/al Qaeda connection. *Social Semiotics, 17*(1), 5–20.

Holstein, J. A., & Gubrium, J. F. (2003). Active interviewing. In J. F. Gubrium & J. A. Holstein (Eds.), *Postmodern interviewing* (pp. 67–80). Thousand Oaks, CA: Sage.

Kamberelis, G., & Dimitriadis, G. (2005). Focus groups: Strategic articulations of pedagogy, politics and inquiry. In N. K. Denzin & Y. S. Lincoln (Eds.), *The Sage handbook of qualitative research* (3rd ed., pp. 887–914). Thousand Oaks, CA: Sage.

Kaufmann, J. (2005). Autotheory: An autoethnographic reading of Foucault. *Qualitative Inquiry, 11,* 576–587.

Kincheloe, J. L., & McLaren, P. (2005). Rethinking critical theory and qualitative research. In N. K. Denzin & Y. S. Lincoln (Eds.), *The Sage handbook of qualitative research* (3rd ed., pp. 303–342). Thousand Oaks, CA: Sage.

Kirk, J., & Miller, M. (1986). *Reliability and validity in qualitative research.* Beverly Hills, CA: Sage.

Kitzinger, C. (2000). Doing feminist conversation analysis. *Feminism and Psychology, 10*(2), 163–193.

Kitzinger, J. (1994). The methodology of focus groups: The importance of interactions between research participants. *Sociology of Health and Illness, 16*(1), 103–121.

Kitzinger, J. (2004). Audience and readership research. In J. Downing, D. McQuail, P. Schlesinger, & E. Wartella (Eds.), *Handbook of media studies* (pp. 167–181). London: Sage.

Krueger, R. (1998). Moderating focus groups. In D. Morgan & R. Krueger (Eds.), *Focus group kit* (Vol. 4, pp. 1–115). Thousand Oaks, CA: Sage.

Krueger, R., & Casey, M. (2000). *Focus groups* (3rd ed.). Thousand Oaks, CA: Sage.

Kvale, S. (1996). *InterViews: An introduction to qualitative research interviewing.* Thousand Oaks, CA: Sage.

Kvale, S. (2007). *Doing interviews.* Thousand Oaks, CA: Sage.

Labov, W., &Waletzky, J. (1967). Narrative analysis: Oral versions of personal experience. In J. Helm (Ed.), *Essays on the verbal and visual arts* (pp. 12–44). Seattle: University of Washington Press.

Lapadat, J. C. (2000). Problematizing transcription: Purpose, paradigm, and quality. *International Journal of Social Research Methodology, 3*(3), 203–219.

Lapadat, J. C., & Lindsay, A. C. (1999). Transcription in research and practice: From standardization of technique to interpretive positionings. *Qualitative Inquiry, 5*(1), 64–86.

Lather, P. (1993). Fertile obsession: Validity after poststructuralism. *Sociological Quarterly, 34*(4), 673–693.

Lather, P., & Smithies, C. (1997). *Troubling the angels.* Boulder, CO: Westview.

LeCompete, M. D. & Preissle, J. (2003). *Ethnography and qualitative design in educational research* (2nd ed.). San Diego, CA: Academic Press.

Lee, S. (1962). *Who2 biography: Spiderman, cartoon character.* Available online at www.answers.com/topic/spiderman?cat=entertainment (retrieved June 1, 2008).

Leiblich, A., Tuval-Mashiach, R., & Zilber, T. (1998). *Narrative research: Reading, analysis and interpretation for another approach to narrative analysis.* Thousand Oaks, CA: Sage.

Leininger, M. (1985). Ethnoscience method and componential analysis. In M. Leininger (Ed.), *Qualitative research methods in nursing* (pp. 237–249). London: Grune and Stratton.

Leininger, M. (1994). Evaluation criteria and critique of qualitative research studies. In J. M. Morse (Ed.), *Critical issues in qualitative research methods* (pp. 95–115). Newbury Park, CA: Sage.

Letherby, G. (2003). *Feminist research in theory and practice.* Philadelphia: Open University Press.

Liebow, E. (1967). *Tally's corner.* Boston: Little, Brown.

Lim, M. S. C., Hellard, M. E., & Aitken, C. K. (2005). The case of the disappearing teaspoons: Longitudinal cohort study of the displacement of teaspoons in an Australian research institute. *BMJ Medical Publication of the Year, 331*:1498–1500. Available online at http://www.bmj.com/cgi/content/full/331/7531/1498v (retrieved August 11, 2008).

Lincoln, Y. S. (1995). Emerging criteria for quality in qualitative and interpretive research. *Qualitative Inquiry, 1*(3), 275–289.

Lincoln, Y. S., & Guba, E. G. (1985). *Naturalistic inquiry.* Beverly Hills, CA: Sage.

Lincoln, Y. S., & Guba, E. G. (2000). Paradigmatic controversies, contradictions, and emerging confluences. In N. K. Denzin & Y. S. Lincoln (Eds.), *The Sage handbook of qualitative research* (2nd ed., pp. 163–188). Thousand Oaks, CA, Sage.

Lofland, J. A. & Lofland, L. (1984). *Analyzing social settings: A guide to qualitative observation and analysis* (2nd ed.). Belmont, CA: Wadsworth.

Lynch, M. (2000). Against reflexivity as an academic virtue and source of privileged knowledge. *Theory, Culture & Society, 17*(3), 26–54.

Madill, A., Jordan, A., & Shirley, C. (2000). Objectivity and reliability in qualitative analysis: Realist, contextualist and radical constructionist epistemologies. *British Journal of Psychology, 91,* 1–20.

Madriz, E. (2000). Focus groups in feminist research. In N. K. Denzin & Y. S. Lincoln (Eds.), *The Sage handbook of qualitative research* (2nd ed., pp. 835–850). Thousand Oaks, CA: Sage.

Manning, P. K., & Cullum-Swan, B. (1994). Narrative, content and semiotic analysis. In N. K. Denzin & Y. S. Lincoln (Eds.), *The Sage handbook of qualitative research* (pp. 463–477). Thousand Oaks, CA: Sage.

Marcus, G. E. (1994). What comes (just) after "post": The case of ethnography. In N. K. Denzin & Y.S. Lincoln (Eds.), *The handbook of qualitative research* (pp. 563–574). Thousand Oaks, CA: Sage.

Marcus, J. (2001). Orientalism. In P. Atkinson, A. Coffey, S. Delamont, J. Lofland & L. Lofland (Eds.), *Handbook of ethnography* (pp. 109–117). London: Sage.

Marshall, C., & Rossman, G. B. (1995). *Designing qualitative research* (2nd ed.). Thousand Oaks, CA: Sage.

Maxwell, J. A. (1992). Understanding and validity in qualitative research. *Harvard Educational Review, 62*(3), 279–300.

Maxwell, J. A. (1996). *Qualitative research design: An interactive approach.* Thousand Oaks, CA: Sage.

Mayan, M., Gray, E., Richter, S., Drummond, J., & Rebryna, R. (2008). [Families first Edmonton: Document analysis]. Unpublished manuscript, University of Alberta, Edmonton, Canada.

McCubbin, H. K., & Patterson, J. M. (1982). *Family stress, coping and social support.* Springfield, IL: Thomas.

Mead, M. (2001). *Coming of age in Samoa.* City: New York: HarperCollins. (Original work published 1928).

Melhado, E. M. (1998). Economist, public provision, and the market: Changing values in policy debate. *Journal of Health Politics, Policy and Law, 23*(2), 215–263.

Merleau-Ponty, M. (1964). *Signs* (R. C. McClearly, Trans.). Evanston: Northwestern University Press. (Original work published in 1960).

Merleau-Ponty, M. (2002). Phenomenology of perception (Colin Smith, Trans). London: Routledge Classics. (Original work published in 1945).

Merriam, S. B., Johnson-Bailey, J., Lee, M., Kee, Y., Ntseane, G., & Muhamad, M. (2001). Power and positionality: Negotiating insider/outsider status within and across cultures. *International Journal of Lifelong Education, 20*(5), 405–416.

Mishler, E. (1986). *Research interviewing: Context and narrative.* Cambridge, MA: Harvard University Press.

Morgan, D. L. (1997). *Focus groups as qualitative research* (2nd ed.). Thousand Oaks, CA: Sage.

Morgan, D.L. (1998). Planning focus groups. In D. L. Morgan & R. Krueger (Eds.), *Focus group kit* (Vol. 2, pp. 1–139). Thousand Oaks, CA: Sage.

Morgan, D. L., & Krueger, R. (1998). *The focus group kit* (Vols. 1–6). Thousand Oaks, CA: Sage.

Morn, K. H., Patterson, B. J., Kurtz, B., & Brzowski, B. (1999). Mothers' responses to care given by male nursing students during and after Birth. *Image: Journal of Nursing Scholarship, 31*(1), 83–87.

Morse, J. M. (1991a). Qualitative research: A free-for-all? In J. Morse (Ed.), *Qualitative nursing research: A contemporary dialogue* (pp. 14–22). Newbury Park, CA: Sage.

Morse, J. M. (1991b). Strategies for sampling. In J. Morse (Ed.), *Qualitative nursing research: A contemporary dialogue* (Rev. ed., pp. 117–131). Newbury Park, CA: Sage.

Morse, J. M. (1994a). Designing qualitative research. In N. K. Denzin & Y. S. Lincoln (Eds.), *The handbook of qualitative research* (pp. 220–235). Thousand Oaks, CA: Sage.

Morse, J. M. (1994b). Emerging from the data: The cognitive processes of analysis in qualitative inquiry. In Janice M. Morse (Ed.), *Critical issues in qualitative research methods* (pp. 23–43). Thousand Oaks, CA: Sage.

Morse, J. M. (1997). "Perfectly healthy, but dead": The myth of inter-rater reliability [Editorial]. *Qualitative Health Research, 7,* 445–447.

Morse, J. M. (1999a). Myth 19: Qualitative inquiry is not systematic [Editorial]. *Qualitative Health Research, 9,* 573–574.

Morse, J. M. (1999b). Qualitative generalizability [Editorial]. *Qualitative Health Research, 9,* 5–6.

Morse, J. M. (1999c). The armchair walkthrough [Editorial]. *Qualitative Health Research, 9,* 435–436.

Morse, J. M. (2000a). Determining sample size. *Qualitative Health Research, 10,* 3–5.

Morse, J. M. (2000b). Exploring pragmatic utility: Concept analysis by critically appraising the literature. In B. Rodgers & K. Knafl (Eds.), *Concept development in nursing* (pp. 333–352). Philadelphia: W.B. Saunders.

Morse, J. M. (2006). Biased reflections: Principles of sampling and analysis in qualitative enquiry (pp. 53–60). In J. Popay (Ed.), *Moving beyond effectiveness in evidence synthesis: Methodological issues in the synthesis of diverse sources of evidence.* London: HAD.

Morse, J. M., Barrett, M., Mayan, M., Olson K., & Spiers, J. (2002). Verification strategies for establishing reliability and validity in qualitative research. *International Journal of Qualitative Methods, 1*(2), Article 2. Available online at http://www.ualberta.ca/~iiqm/backissues/1_2Final/pdf/ morseetal.pdf (retrieved January 17, 2008).

Morse, J. M., Beres, M., Spiers, J., Mayan, M. J., & Olson, K. (2003). Identifying signals of suffering by linking verbal and facial cues. *Qualitative Health Research, 13,* 1063–1077.

Morse, J. M. & Field, P. A. (1995). *Qualitative research methods for health professionals* (2nd ed.). Thousand Oaks, CA: Sage.

Morse, J. M., Hupcey, J. E., Mitcham, C., & Lenz, E. R. (1997). Choosing a strategy for concept analysis in nursing research: Moving beyond Wilson. In A. G. Gift (Ed.), *Clarifying concepts in nursing research* (pp. 73–96). New York: Springer.

Morse, J. M., Mitcham, C., Hupcey, J. E., & Tason, M. (1996). Criteria for concept evaluation. *Journal of Advanced Nursing Practice, 24,* 385–390.

Morse, J. M., & Niehaus, L. (2007). Combining qualitative and quantitative methods for mixed method designs. In P. Munhall (Ed.), *Nursing research: A qualitative perspective* (4th ed., pp. 541–554). Boston: Jones & Bartlett.

Morse, J. M., Niehaus, L. Varnhagen, S., Austin, W., & McIntosh, M. (2008). Qualitative researchers' conceptualizations of the risks inherent in qualitative interviews. *International Review of Qualitative Research, 1*(2), 195–214.

Morse, J. M., Stern, P., Corbin, J. M., Charmaz, K. C., Bowers, B., & Clarke, A. E. (2008). *Developing grounded theory.* Walnut Creek, CA: Left Coast Press.

Olson, K., Krawchuk, A., & Quddusi, T. (2007). Fatigue in individuals with advanced cancer in active treatment and palliative settings. *Cancer Nursing, 30*(4), E1–E10.

Paley, J., & Eva, G. (2005). Narrative vigilance: The analysis of stories on health care. *Nursing Philosophy, 6,* 83–97.

Patai, D. (1994). When method becomes power [Response]. In A. Gitlen (Ed.), *Power and method: Political activism and education research* (pp. 61–73). New York: Routledge.

Patton, M. (2002). *Qualitative research and evaluation methods* (3rd ed.). Thousand Oaks, CA: Sage.

Piantanida, M., & Garman, N. B. (1999). *The qualitative dissertation.* Thousand Oaks, CA: Sage.

Pillow, W. S. (2003). Confession, catharsis, or cure?: Rethinking the uses of reflexivity as methodological power in qualitative research. *Qualitative Studies in Education, 16*(2), 175–196.

Pink, S. (2007). *Doing visual ethnography* (2nd ed.). Thousand Oaks, CA: Sage.

Poland, B. D. (1995). Transcription quality as an aspect of rigor in qualitative research. *Qualitative Inquiry, 1*(3), 290–310.

Polkinghorne, D. (1983). *Methodology for the human sciences.* Albany, NY: SUNY Press.

Popay, J., Rogers, A., & Williams, G. (1998). Rationale and standards for the systematic review of qualitative literature in health services research. *Qualitative Health Research, 8,* 341–351.

Princen, T., Maniates, M., & Conca, K. (2002). (Eds). *Confronting consumption.* Cambridge, MA: MIT Press.

Rabinow, P. (1977). *Reflections on fieldwork in Morocco.* Berkeley: University of California Press.

Ray, L., & Mayan, M. (2001). Who decides what counts as evidence? In J. M. Morse, J. M. Swanson, & A. J. Kuzel (Eds.), *The nature of qualitative evidence* (pp. 50–73). Thousand Oaks, CA: Sage.

Reed-Danahay, D. E. (1997). *Auto/Ethnography: Rewriting the self and the social.* Oxford, UK: Berg.

Richards, L., & Morse, J. M. (2007). *Readme first for a user's guide to qualitative methods* (2nd ed.). Thousand Oaks, CA: Sage.

Richardson, L. (2000). Evaluating ethnography. *Qualitative Inquiry, 6*(2), 253–255.

Richardson, L. (2007). *Last Writes: A daybook for a dying friend.* Walnut Creek, CA: Left Coast Press.

Richardson, L., & St. Pierre, E. A. (2005). Writing: A method of inquiry. In N. K. Denzin & Y. S. Lincoln (Eds.), *The Sage handbook of qualitative research* (3rd ed., pp. 959–978). Thousand Oaks, CA: Sage.

Rubin, H. J., & Rubin, I. S. (1995). *Qualitative interviewing: The art of hearing data.* Thousand Oaks, CA: Sage.

Rubin, H. J., & Rubin, I. S. (2005). *Qualitative interviewing: The art of hearing data* (2nd ed.). Thousand Oaks, CA: Sage.

Sacks, H. (1992). *Lectures on conversation.* (G. Jefferson, Ed.). Cambridge, MA: Blackwell Publishing.

Said, E. (1978). *Orientalism.* New York: Pantheon.

Sandelowski, M. (2000). Whatever happened to qualitative description? *Research in Nursing and Health, 23*, 334–340.

Sandelowski, M., & Barroso, J. (2002). Reading qualitative studies. *International Journal for Qualitative Methods, 1*(1), Article 5. Available online at http://www.ualberta.ca/~iiqm/backissues/1_1Final/pdf/ sandeleng.pdf (retrieved July 15, 2007).

Sandelowski, M., & Barroso, J. (2003). Writing the proposal for a qualitative research methodology project. *Qualitative Health Research, 13*, 781–820.

Sandelowski, M., & Corson Jones, L. (1996). Healing fictions: Stories of choosing in the aftermath of the detection of fetal anomalies. *Social Science and Medicine, 42*(3), 353–361.

Schensul, S., Schensul, J., & LeCompte, M. D. (1999). *Essential ethnographic methods: Observations, interviews, and questionnaires.* Walnut Creek, CA: AltaMira.

Schutz, A. (1967). *The phenomenology of the social world* (G. Walsh & F. Lehnert, Trans.). Evanston, IL: Northwestern University Press. (Original work published in 1932).

Seale, C. (1999). *The quality of qualitative research.* London: Sage.

Sherif, B. (2001). The ambiguity of boundaries in the fieldwork experience: Establishing rapport and negotiating insider/outside status. *Qualitative Inquiry, 7,* 436–447.

Sherman Heyl, B. (2001). Ethnographic interviewing. In P. Atkinson, A. Coffey, S. Delamont, J. Lofland, & L. Lofland (Eds.), *Handbook of ethnography* (pp. 369–383). Thousand Oaks, CA: Sage.

Silverman, D. (1998). *Interpreting qualitative data: Strategies for analyzing talk, text and interaction.* London: Sage.

Skeggs, B. (1994). Situating the production of feminist ethnography. In M. Maynard & J. Purvis (Eds.), *Researching women's lives from a feminist perspective* (pp. 72–92). London: Taylor and Francis.

Smith, G. C. S., & Pell, J. P. (2003). Parachute use to prevent death and major trauma related to gravitational challenge: Systematic review of randomised controlled trials. *BMJ Medical Publication of the Year, 327,* 1459–1461. Available online at http://www.bmj.com/cgi/content/full/327/7429/1459 (retrieved August 12, 2008),

Smith, S. E., Willms, D. G., & Johnson, N. A. (Eds.). (1997). *Nurtured by knowledge: Learning to do participatory action research* (pp. xi–xii). New York: Apex.

Sparkes, A. C. (1996). The fatal flaw: A narrative of the fragile body-self. *Qualitative Inquiry, 2,* 463–494.

Sparkes, A. C. (2000). Autoethnography and narratives of self: Reflections on criteria in action. *Sociology of Sport Journal, 17*(1), 21–43.

Spradley, J. P. (1979). *The ethnographic interview.* Fort Worth, TX: Harcourt Brace Jovanovich College.

Stake, R. E. (2005). Qualitative case studies. In N. K. Denzin & Y. S. Lincoln (Eds.), *The Sage handbook of qualitative research* (3rd ed., pp. 443–466). Thousand Oaks, CA: Sage.

Stoecker, R. (2004, May). Creative tensions in the new community based research. Keynote address presented at the Community-Based Research Network Symposium, Carleton University, Ottawa, Canada. Available online at http://comm-org.wisc.edu/drafts/cbrtensions.htm (retrieved March 23, 2007).Thomas, J. (1993). *Doing critical ethnography.* Newbury Park, CA: Sage.

Thorne, S. (1997). The art (and science) of critiquing qualitative research. In J. Morse (Ed.), *Completing a qualitative project: Details and dialogue* (pp. 117–132). Thousand Oaks, CA: Sage.

Thorne, S. (2008). *Interpretive description.* Walnut Creek, CA: Left Coast Press.

Thorne, S., Kirkham, R. S., & O'Flynn-Magee, K. (2004). The analytic challenge in interpretive description. *International Journal of Qualitative Methods, 3*(1), Article 1. Available online at http://www.ualberta.ca/~iiqm/backissues/3_1/pdf/thorneetal.pdf (retrieved February 20, 2007).

Thorne, S., McGinness, L., McPherson, G., Con, A., Cunningham, M., & Harris, S. (2004). Health care communication issues in fibromyalgia: An interpretive description. *Physiotherapy Canada, 56*(1), 31–38.

Tilley, S. (2003). "Challenging" research practices: Turning a critical lens on the work of transcription. *Qualitative Inquiry, 9*(5), 750–773.

Tourigny, S. C. (1998). Some new dying trick: African American youths "choosing" HIV/AIDS. *Qualitative Health Research, 8,* 149–167.

van den Hoonaard, W. C. (2002). *Walking the tightrope.* Toronto, Canada: University of Toronto Press.

Van Maanen, J. (1988). *Tales of the field: On writing ethnography.* Chicago: University of Chicago Press.

van Manen, M. (1997). *Researching lived experience: Human science for an action sensitive pedagogy.* London, Canada: Althouse.

van Manen, M. (2001). *Researching lived experience: Human science for an action sensitive pedagogy* (2nd ed.). London, Canada: Althouse.

Wall, D. (2002). Dissent among the faithful: Conflict and its management within selected Christian denominations—A comparative analysis. Master's thesis, Royal Roads University, Victoria, Canada. *Masters Abstracts International, 41*(2), 392.

Wall, S. (2006). An autoethnography on learning about autoethnography. *International Journal of Qualitative Methods, 5*(2), Article 9. Available online at http://www.ualberta.ca/~iiqm/backissues/5_2/HTML/wall.htm (retrieved February 20, 2007).

Wang, C. C., Burris, M. A., & Ping, X. Y. (1996). Chinese village women as visual anthropologists: A participatory approach to reaching policymakers. *Social Science & Medicine, 42*(10), 1391–1400.

Wang, C. C., Morrel-Samuels, S., Hutchison, P. M., Bell, L., & Pestronk, R. M. (2004). Flint photovoice: Community building among youths, adults, and policymakers. *American Journal of Public Health, 94*(6), 911–913.

Weaver, K., & Morse, J. M. (2006). Pragmatic utility: Using analytical questions to explore the concept of ethical sensitivity. *Research and Theory for Nursing Practice: An International Journal, 20*(3), 191–214.

Wetherell, M. (2001). Debates in discourse research. In M. Wetherell, S. Taylor, & S. J. Yates (Eds.), *Discourse theory and practice* (pp. 380–399). London: Sage.

Wilkinson, S. (1988). The role of reflexivity in feminist psychology. *Women's Studies International Forum, 11,* 493–502.

Wilkinson, S. (1999). How useful are focus groups in feminist research? In J. K. Kitzinger & R. S. Barbour (Eds), *Developing focus group research* (pp. 64–78). London: Sage.

Willis, G. B. (2005). *Cognitive interviewing: A tool for improving questionnaire design.* Thousand Oaks, CA: Sage.

Wills, B. S. H. (2005). *The responses of the elderly Chinese in Edmonton to the threat of SARS.* Doctoral dissertation, University of Alberta, Edmonton, Canada. *Dissertation Abstracts International, 66*(10), 5327B.

Wittgenstein, L. (1969). *Notebooks, 1914–1916* (G.E.M. Anscombe, Trans.). New York: Harper. (Original work published in 1961).

Woolgar, S. (1988). Reflexivity is the ethnographer of the text. In S. Woolgar (Ed.), *New frontiers in the sociology of knowledge* (pp. 14–34). London: Sage.

Wuest, J., Merritt-Gray, M., & Ford-Gilboe, M. (2004). Regenerating family: Strengthening the emotional health of mothers and children in the context of intimate partner violence. *Advances in Nursing Science, 27*(4), 257–274.

# Index

# About the Author

Maria J. Mayan is a qualitative methodologist and has studied, written about, and conducted qualitative research since the early 1990s. She spent over ten years at the International Institute for Qualitative Methodology learning and teaching qualitative inquiry locally and internationally. She is currently an associate professor in the Faculty of Extension and assistant director of Women's and Children's Health, Community University Partnership for the Study of Children, Youth and Families, University of Alberta. She has been invited to teach qualitative inquiry by the government, not-for-profits, the private sector, and the academic community worldwide. Her research program is primarily community based, focusing on partnerships and health policy.